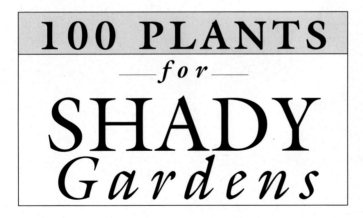

100 PLANTS
for
SHADY
Gardens

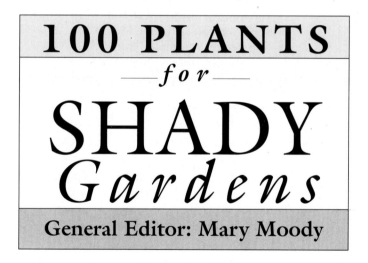

100 PLANTS
for
SHADY
Gardens

General Editor: Mary Moody

CRESCENT BOOKS

NEW YORK • AVENEL

Contributing writers: Mary Moody, Stephanie Watson

Published by Lansdowne Publishing Pty Ltd
Level 5, 70 George Street, Sydney NSW 2000, Australia

This 1995 edition published by Crescent Books,
distributed by Random House Value Publishing, Inc.,
40 Engelhard Avenue, Avenel, New Jersey 07001

Random House
New York • Toronto • London • Sydney • Auckland

First published 1994

Managing Director: Jane Curry
Publishing Manager: Deborah Nixon
Production Manager: Sally Stokes
Project Coordinator: Kate Oliver
Copy Editor: Doug Cooper
Horticultural Advisor: Liz Ball
Design Concept: Catherine Martin
Typesetter: Veronica Hilton
Formatted in Galliard on Quark Xpress
Printed in Singapore by Kyodo Printing Co (S'pore) Pte Ltd

ISBN 0-517-12126-3

A CIP catalog record for this book is available from the Library of Congress.

KEY TO SYMBOLS

◐	prefers partial shade
●	prefers full shade
pH̬	acid soil
p̂H	alkaline soil
❖	half-hardy – temperatures down to 0°C
❖❖	hardy – temperatures down to -5°C
❖❖❖	fully hardy – temperatures down to -15°C

Contents

76, 79 80 90

Introduction

❀ **GARDENING IN THE DARK** Every garden has at least one area that is shady, perhaps where a canopy of established trees blocks direct sunlight to the understorey, or where the house or other buildings caste a shadow for some hours of the day. Other gardens, especially in areas with little winter sunshine, are predominantly shady, and this can pose problems for those gardeners who wish to introduce colour and texture to the landscape in areas that appear dark and dreary.

Although shade is a welcome relief in the heat of summer, too often shady areas of the garden are bare and denuded of vegetation, which can make them unappealing. With some thought and planning it is easy to cultivate a fertile garden even in these dark corners, taking into account the demands of this special environment and the types of plants that are best suited to the growing conditions.

❀ **DEFINING SHADE** Dark areas of the garden can be caused by various situations, including large trees with spreading branches or buildings, walls and fences that cast a permanent shadow on one particular patch. In warm or hot climates the shade will probably have been deliberately created, to cool the house and outdoor living areas, by using either a deep verandah or pergola covered with climbing plants, or by the planting of large shade trees to create a cool green canopy. Some areas are shaded for only a few hours of the day, while others have the benefit of dappled sunlight filtering through overhanging trees, shrubs or climbers. The way in which you approach sh.ade gardening will depend on two major factors—the degree of shade and the soil conditions of the area where you are planning to create the shady garden.

Shade beneath established trees: These areas of the garden are notoriously dry and hard to cultivate because established trees generally have a thick root system that depletes the soil around the base. The roots not only compete for moisture and nutrients, but can take up most of the available ground space making cultivation extremely difficult. A lot of work will be needed to improve the soil if plants or grasses are to survive in these unfavourable conditions. One method is to create built-up beds using plenty of well-rotted compost, manures and other organic matter to create a reasonable growing environment for the understorey. Depending on the species of tree that make up the canopy, this can be quite successful, although eventually some of the tree roots are bound to travel upwards in search of nutrients and moisture in the garden beds. It is important, therefore, to always water these shady areas deeply to encourage the downward growth of roots. It is also important to select plants that do not mind competing with the trees.

Shaded by the house: Narrow pathways down the side of the house can look dark and dreary due to lack of sun. Yet it is possible to make the most of these conditions to create a lush garden with ground covers and other hardy species in every nook and cranny. The house will also provide plenty of shelter from gusty winds, making these situations ideal for plants that need cool, dark and protected positions. One of the main problems with garden beds adjoining the house is the lack of water due to overhanging eaves. During rain, the rest of the garden gets a good soaking, while these areas stay dry. One solution is to install a small automatic watering system with a series of fine spray outlets that will provide water once or twice a week, depending on the climate. The soil here too is often less than ideal, having been compacted by the building, or depleted after long periods without moisture. The addition of plenty of organic matter will help to remedy this situation, together with mulching which will help the soil to retain moisture after watering.

Dappled shade: Areas of dappled shade are more restful and soothing than either full sun or full shade. So many species thrive in dappled light that it is well worth planning and planting a special bed if you have such an area in your garden. Most ferns, for example, love dappled shade, and this can be an ideal location for a series of hanging baskets, or even a fern garden if the soil and climate permits. This is also an ideal place for a woodland garden, planted with bulbs and other species that easily naturalize beneath the spread of deciduous trees. Again, the soil in this situation can sometimes be sadly lacking in moisture and nutrients, and will require building up with humus to make it a more suitable environment for planting.

Semi-shade: This is a term often used in gardening books, referring to areas that are shaded for part of the day only. There are a great many plants that thrive in this situation, especially those that appreciate a little protection from the glaring sun in the middle of the day during summer. Generally, plants that grow well in semi-shade require just sufficient sunlight to produce flowers. This can be as a little as two hours a day, according to the species.

Deep shade: This is the most difficult area to work with, because there are so few species that really enjoy low light levels. Certainly there are quite a few foliage plants that will grow well without the benefit of bright light, but plants that produce flowers invariably need some brightness to bring on the blooms.

❀ **CREATING A SHADY GARDEN** To successfully garden in shaded areas, always make sure that the soil has been built up with plenty of organic matter, such as well-rotted manure and compost, and water well – even during winter – to prevent the ground from drying out. In some areas, peat may need to be added to create the right growing conditions, especially for plants that have a specific requirement for soil that holds moisture well in summer. Shady gardens should also be well mulched so that they will not dry out as quickly, and less watering will therefore be required.

Growing plants in containers can be particularly useful when creating a shady garden. For instance, plants in containers can be positioned strategically beneath trees to add brightness and beauty in areas where the soil is depleted. This is ideal for gardeners who live in cool and cold areas, where harsh winters will not suit a great many plants. In this situation, the more tender varieties can be taken under cover in late autumn, then brought out to provide a wonderful display in spring. It also solves the problem of soil that does not suit the plants you wish to grow. There are many gardens with alkaline soil where popular plants such as camellias, rhododendrons and azaleas cannot grow. However, these shade lovers can be successfully cultivated in tubs and pots with potting soil that has an acid pH level, then dotted around the garden to brighten up dark and dreary corners.

❀ **THE RIGHT PLANTS** To get good results when gardening in the shade, always select species that are suited to this particular situation. Plants that are grown away from their ideal climate, soil or light requirement, usually fail to thrive and become much more susceptible to infestation by pests and disease. When selecting plants, first establish if they are suited to your local climate, especially in areas that experience very cold winters. Finally, create the soil conditions that are correct for each plant, adding extra humus where required. Also, take note of individual watering requirements as some species, especially bulbs, do not enjoy being overwatered during their dormancy.

✿ HOW TO USE THIS BOOK

This book has been designed as a simple guide to successfully cultivating all the plants listed. The soil pH level has been specified only when it needs to be either acid or alkaline, according to the particular requirements of the plant. All other plants can be easily grown in soil in the neutral range (that is, pH 7.0). Refer to the key to symbols on page 4.

A plant's preference for partial shade or full shade, and its hardiness rating are also indicated by symbols. The hardiness symbols indicate each individual plant's ability to withstand winter temperatures and frost. No symbols have been given for annuals, which are only grown from spring to autumn in cool and cold climates, and therefore are not expected to survive winter.

The mature height of plants, indicated under 'Description', may vary from one climate to another, sometimes only reaching the maximum size in the country in which it is a native species.

Where advice has been given on pests and disease infestations, this is meant as a guide to a certain plant's susceptibility to a particular problem. Treatment of that problem will vary from one country to another.

Achimenes grandiflora

Big purple achimenes ◑ ● ❖

❀ **OTHER NAME** Hot water plant ❀ **DESCRIPTION** A handsome, erect perennial that grows and spreads to 2 feet (60 cm) with tuber-like rhizomes that make it easy to propagate. In cold climates this plant can be grown in a container indoors or in a greenhouse and moved outside in the warmer months. It likes high light levels but not direct sunlight, which can damage the sensitive flowers and foliage. A native of Mexico, it has oval leaves with a toothed edge, which are reddish on the underside. The flowers are large and tubular, pink-purple in colour, with a white eye. ❀ **PLANTING** Good drainage is essential for healthy growth, either in the ground or in a container. The soil should be moderately rich and capable of retaining moisture. ❀ **FLOWERING** Flowers appear in summer. ❀ **CULTIVATION** Water routinely during hot or dry weather but reduce watering after flowering and store rhizomes in shelter over winter where the climate is cold. ❀ **PROPAGATION** Either by division of rhizomes in early spring or by seed sown in spring. Stem cuttings can also be taken in summer.

Actaea pachypoda (syn. *Actaea alba*)

White baneberry ◑ pH ❖❖❖

✿ **DESCRIPTION** *Actaeas* are related to the common ranunculus but differ insofar as they are generally grown for their delightful but poisonous autumn berries. White baneberries are clump-forming perennials and normally grow to a height of 3 feet (90 cm), spreading 18 inches (45 cm). Their flowering spikes appear during summer and bear a handsome display of dainty, pure-white flowers which are fluffy in appearance. Soon after, decorative clusters of white berries follow, which look dramatic against the upright, scarlet stalks. The leaves are serrated, deeply divided, and emerge at ground level. White baneberries are best suited to woodland gardens.

✿ **PLANTING** Spring and autumn are the best times to plant, and all but the coldest areas are suitable. Choose a site with dappled shade and rich, moist, woodland soil for best results. If necessary, enrich the soil with peat or well-rotted compost prior to planting. ✿ **FLOWERING** Flowers appear during summer and are promptly followed by a mass of autumn berries. ✿ **CULTIVATION** *Actaeas* are frost resistant but cannot tolerate drought, so mulch well during summer with leaf litter. Prune during late autumn. ✿ **PROPAGATION** Divide and replant clumps during early spring or sow fresh seed during autumn or spring.

Ajuga reptans

Bugle

◑ ● ❖❖❖

❀ **OTHER NAME** Carpet bugle, Bugleweed ❀ **DESCRIPTION** A popular, creeping perennial with a semi-evergreen habit. *Ajuga reptans* is ideal for the shaded garden and looks most attractive when planted around shrubs, in rockeries, or between garden steps. The original species produces mounded rosettes up to 6 inches (15 cm) high, with shiny green leaves that turn burgundy during autumn. The foliage of new cultivars varies, however, from crimson through to bronze. During spring, compact and erect flower spikes emerge in shades of blue, white or pink.There is also a giant form available. ❀ **PLANTING** Plant during spring into any soil type, provided it is moist and well drained. Poorer soils can be enriched at planting time with the addition of compost and pulverized manure. *Ajugas* do not like to dry out, so choose a shaded position and place new plants at 6–12 inches (15-30 cm) intervals. ❀ **FLOWERING** Flowers appear from spring through to summer. ❀ **CULTIVATION** Never allow the soil to dry out, particularly through the warmer months. A light dressing of complete fertilizer during early spring will ensure a good crop of flowers. Remove blooms as they wither and keep an eye open for any fungal diseases. ❀ **PROPAGATION** Runners can be divided at any time but preferably during spring.

Alchemilla mollis

Lady's mantle ◑ ❖❖❖

✿ **DESCRIPTION** For a splash of summer gold, the lady's mantle is a difficult plant to surpass. It is a charming, ground-covering species that is well suited for rock gardens, perennial borders, or pool sides, where its silhouette reflects in the water. A perennial with a clump-forming habit, the lady's mantle thrives in moist, shaded areas and grows to a height of 16 inches (40 cm) with a similar spread. There soft, tomentose leaves with scalloped edges closely resemble the capes worn by ladies at the turn of the century. When in flower, the plant becomes smothered by a profusion of tiny greenish-gold, petalless flowers, which are useful for dried flower arrangements. ✿ **PLANTING** Choose a lightly shaded position with moist, well-drained soil. Plant in autumn or spring, setting plants approximately 15 inches (38 cm) apart. ✿ **FLOWERING** Sprays of tiny golden flowers appear during summer that self-seed freely in autumn. ✿ **CULTIVATION** Keep moist at all times and mulch generously during the warmer months. During dry weather mulch well to prevent the soil from drying out rapidly. Feed each spring with an application of well-rotted manure. After seeding, cut back to just above ground level. ✿ **PROPAGATION** Transplant self-sown seedlings or divide larger specimens during autumn or spring.

Anemone blanda
Windflower ◑ ❖❖❖

❀ **OTHER NAME** Greek Anemone ❀ **DESCRIPTION** *Anemone blanda* is a charming little member of the Ranunculaceae family and thrives in the shade of large, deciduous trees. Its flattened blooms come in pastel shades of pink, white, or blue, measuring 2 inches (5 cm) across, and are abundant from late winter to early spring. This captivating perennial plant emerges surprisingly from an ugly, knobbly tuber. *A. blanda* has a spreading habit and grows to a modest height of 4 inches (10 cm). Its leaves are dark green and finely divided. There are many worthwhile varieties including 'White splendour', which has white flowers, and 'Blue pearl', which has clear blue flowers with yellow stamens. ❀ **PLANTING** Plant tubers at 6 inch (15 cm) intervals during early winter into moist, well-drained, humus-rich soil. A protected, partly shaded position is essential. Begin watering in earnest when the foliage first appears. ❀ **FLOWERING** Depending on climate, flowers appear from late winter to early spring, producing seed in late summer. ❀ **CULTIVATION** Keep moist throughout the growing season and apply a dressing of complete fertilizer during early spring to boost the new growth. In autumn cut plants back to ground level and allow the tubers to remain undisturbed. Lift and divide tubers only when they have become overcrowded. ❀ **PROPAGATION** By division in spring or by sowing fresh seed in late summer.

Anemone nemorosa

Windflower ◕ ❖❖❖

✿ **OTHER NAME** European wood anemone

✿ **DESCRIPTION** *Anemone nemorosa* is a great lover of woodland conditions. It is a vigorous spreading perennial that reaches a height of 6 inches (15 cm) and emerges from a long, thin, creeping rhizome. From late spring to early summer, a mass of singular, white, star-shaped blooms appear, with rosy-pink undersides and conspicuous yellow stamens. The mid-green leaves are tri-lobed, deeply divided and lance-shaped. During autumn, rounded clusters of hairy nutlets appear that contain the seed.

✿ **PLANTING** Set the rhizomes out during early winter into moist, peaty soil with good drainage. An area beneath a deciduous tree is ideal, as it will provide the necessary dappled shade. Space rhizomes 12 inches (30 cm) apart and bury them at a depth of 2 inches (5 cm). ✿ **FLOWERING** A profusion of blooms appears from late spring to early summer. ✿ **CULTIVATION** *Anemone nemorosa* is susceptible to drought conditions, so keep it moist during spring and summer. An application of organic mulch will reduce the need for watering. Feed during early spring with complete fertilizer, and in late autumn prune back to ground level. Avoid lifting the rhizomes except for the purposes of propagation. ✿ **PROPAGATION** By root cuttings taken during winter or by seed sown in autumn.

Aquilegia caerulea

Columbine ⦿ ṗH ❖❖❖

✿ **OTHER NAME** Colorado columbine ✿ **DESCRIPTION** *Aquilegia caerulea* is Colorado's floral emblem and is also the parent of many highly sought after, long-spurred cultivars. Columbines look most effective in cottage-style gardens and alpine rockeries, or when planted amongst other herbaceous perennials. This particular species grows 1½–2 feet (45–60 cm) tall and produces large blue and white flowers. Their thin, fern-like leaves arise from basal clumps and gradually wither and die after the flowering process has finished. If permitted, columbines will self-seed freely throughout the garden but may not always grow true to type. There are many fascinating hybrids with flowers ranging from white to creamy-yellow, blue-purple and crimson. ✿ **PLANTING** Choose a position with light shade and moist, well-drained, alkaline soil. Seeds can be sown direct in spring and later thinned out, or alternatively, seedlings may be planted at 14 inch (35 cm) intervals during autumn. Be sure to plant seedlings with the crown just above soil level. ✿ **FLOWERING** From early to late spring, depending on climate, for a month or so. ✿ **CULTIVATION** In late autumn, when the plants begin to die, cut them back almost to ground level. For larger blooms, feed throughout the growing season with liquid fertilizer. Keep them well watered and watch for aphid attacks. ✿ **PROPAGATION** By seed in early spring or division in autumn.

Astilbe arendsii

Hybrid astilbe ◑ ❖❖❖

✿ **DESCRIPTION** For midsummer hues, hybrid astilbes are hard to beat with their graceful, spire-like plumes in various shades of white, pink, and red. The shining, compounded leaves are handsome too. When young, they develop attractive, coppery tones, reverting to dark green at maturity. For maximum impact, plant en masse in a rockery, under a large tree, or by the poolside where they will relish the moist conditions. The flowering stems can reach between 2–3 feet (60–90 cm) and look magnificent in vase arrangements. When left to their own devices however, astilbes set seed in autumn. ✿ **PLANTING** The site should be lightly shaded with deep, moist soil, rich in organic matter. Space plants 2 feet (60 cm) apart during early spring and water in well. ✿ **FLOWERING** For a period of two months during midsummer. ✿ **CULTIVATION** Every two to three years, lift and divide the clumps during spring and enrich the soil with copious quantities of organic matter. Astilbes must be kept moist throughout the growing season but drier during their dormant phase. In late autumn, cut the foliage back to ground level. ✿ **PROPAGATION** By seed in autumn or division in early spring.

peran, —   *12–16"*

Begonia rex

Painted leaf begonia ◑ pH ❖

❧ **DESCRIPTION** In cold climates this evergreen perennial can be
grown outdoors in a container, then brought inside as a houseplant in
winter. Although *Begonia rex* produces small, pale pink flowers, the plant is
prized for its striking, metallic foliage. Its often hairy leaves are shaped like
elephant's ears and come in beautiful shades of green, bronze, red, silver, or
pink, and nearly all varieties are multicoloured with delicate patterns.
Begonia rex looks stunning when grown in bedding displays, pots, or
hanging baskets. It normally reaches a height of 12–16 inches (30–40 cm).
❧ **PLANTING** Choose a sheltered site, protected from the strong
afternoon sun and plant into rich, slightly acidic, well-drained soil. Indoors,
use a quality potting mix and keep out of direct sunlight or draughts.
❧ **FLOWERING** Sporadically from late winter through to summer.
❧ **CULTIVATION** Water sparingly and avoid wetting the foliage.
Pruning is not necessary except for the removal of the flowers to encourage
stronger, healthier foliage. Feed fortnightly with liquid fertilizer throughout
the growing season and watch for fungal diseases. ❧ **PROPAGATION**
By leaf cuttings in late spring and division in summer or autumn.

Bergenia cordifolia

Heart-leaf bergenia ❂ ❖❖❖

❀ **DESCRIPTION** A useful bedding plant for the home garden is the heart-leaf bergenia with its attractive, large, rounded, leathery leaves, and sweetly perfumed, nodding, pink blooms. They grow to a conservative height of 6 inches (15 cm) and look best when planted along the edge of perennial borders or under the canopy of tall trees or shrubs. Heart-leaf bergenias are hardy, evergreen perennials and require very little attention. The flowers are borne on stout stems that barely extend beyond the leaves. Even when they have faded, the leaves provide year-round interest, particularly in cooler climates where they turn bronze in winter. ❀ **PLANTING** Bergenias thrive in most soil types, will tolerate some sun, but prefer light shade. Set new plants out at 15 inch (38 cm) intervals. ❀ **FLOWERING** Flowers appear in succession from early spring and last for a month. ❀ **CULTIVATION** When clumps become overcrowded, lift and divide during autumn. Remove spent flowers to prolong the flowering season and, periodically, any damaged or dying leaves. Keep moist throughout summer and feed annually with a general fertilizer. Mulching is also beneficial. Slug and snail control is a must. ❀ **PROPAGATION** By division of mature clumps in autumn or by seed.

peren, - / "

Campanula carpatica
Bellflower ◑ ❖❖❖

✿ **OTHER NAME** Carpathian bellflower ✿ **DESCRIPTION** This pretty, clump-forming perennial is often grown as a ground-covering plant in shady and sheltered parts of the garden. Growing to 1 foot (30 cm) in height, it forms a pleasant mound of mid-green rounded or oval-toothed foliage. The flowers are the main feature of the plant, being showy and bell shaped in the violet-blue to white range. A compact dwarf form, 'Blue Carpet', is a good specimen for a container, while the variety 'Bressingham White' has outstanding pure white bellflowers. ✿ **PLANTING** To produce good results, ensure that the soil is rich, moist, and well drained, with some additional compost incorporated prior to planting. Best results are achieved in partial shade with some protection from strong winds, especially during summer. ✿ **FLOWERING** Flowers for several weeks during summer. ✿ **CULTIVATION** Water routinely during spring and summer, then reduce watering when conditions become cooler. Mulch to keep weed growth to a minimum. ✿ **PROPAGATION** Either from seed sown in spring, division of clumps in autumn, or from softwood cuttings taken in summer.

Chelone obliqua
Turtle head ◐ ❖❖❖

✿ **DESCRIPTION** An easy and delightful plant to grow in a shady spot is the turtle head, with spikes of fascinating, purplish-pink blooms that very much resemble its namesake. Its flowers contrast beautifully with the lightly serrated, dark green, lance-shaped leaves. They are perennials and grow to a useful height of 2–3 feet (60–90 cm). Turtle heads can withstand light frosts but detest dry conditions. Pests and diseases are rarely a problem.

✿ **PLANTING** Grow in a protected, partially shaded area with rich, moist soil. Prior to planting, incorporate generous amounts of well-rotted compost and manure into the soil to improve its water-holding capacity. Young specimens get off to a flying start when planted in spring and should be spaced at 18 inch (45 cm) intervals. ✿ **FLOWERING** Flowering commences in late summer and continues throughout autumn when many other shrubs are beyond their best. Each spike produces a succession of blooms over a two-month period. ✿ **CULTIVATION** Water generously throughout summer and mulch well. Prune lightly after flowering to maintain a bushy appearance and divide clumps every few years. ✿ **PROPAGATION** By soft-tip cuttings during summer, or by division, or seed in autumn or spring.

Cornus canadensis

Creeping dogwood   ◔ pH ❖❖❖

❀ **OTHER NAME** Bunchberry ❀ **DESCRIPTION** A delightful, ground-covering perennial that is ideal for woodland gardens or shady areas beneath the spread of deciduous trees. It is a hardy evergreen plant, with whorls of mid-green oval leaves and small greenish-yellow flowers inside showy white bracts, and grows well in most soil and climates. The flowers are followed by attractive, edible red berries. It grows no more than 6 inches (15 cm) in height and spreads rapidly when grown in the right situation.
❀ **PLANTING** Like many woodland plants, it appreciates moderately rich, moist and well-drained soil conditions. Add some organic matter, such as leaf litter, to the ground prior to planting, and water well until established.
❀ **FLOWERING** Flowers appear during late spring and early summer, followed by the berries. ❀ **CULTIVATION** Keep the ground well watered in spring and summer, especially if conditions are hot and dry.
PROPAGATION By division in spring or autumn.

Cyclamen hederifolium

Neapolitan cyclamen ◑ ❖❖❖

✿ **DESCRIPTION** Every autumn, the delicate blooms of the Neapolitan cyclamen reveal their little heads like a welcome breath of fresh air. Compared to their highly nurtured relatives, these tuberous perennials demand very little attention. Ivy-shaped leaves with silvery-green markings provide a complementary backdrop for the miniature, pale to deep pink, shuttlecock-like blooms. Normally, however, the flowers are first to be seen. During summer the tubers lie dormant in the soil. Neapolitan cyclamens rarely exceed 4 inches (10 cm) in height but can spread up to 6 inches (15 cm).

✿ **PLANTING** New tubers are best planted out in midsummer, into moist, compost-enriched soil. A shady position is essential. Space each tuber from 6 to 8 inches (15 to 20 cm) apart and bury at a depth of 2 inches (5 cm). An organic mulch will protect them from the intense summer heat.

✿ **FLOWERING** Flowers provide a splash of colour throughout autumn and last for several weeks. ✿ **CULTIVATION** Top-dress the garden bed each summer with leaf litter. Keep moist throughout the growing period, but on the dry side while dormant. Disturb only for propagation purposes. Remove spent blooms by twisting them at the base, as well as the foliage when it has completely died back. ✿ **PROPAGATION** By corm division in summer.

Dicentra spectabilis
Common bleeding heart ◑ ❖❖❖

✿ **DESCRIPTION** The charm of the bleeding heart is hard to resist, as its pendent, heart-shaped blooms of white and lipstick-pink appear in spring. This useful plant is a herbaceous perennial, growing to 2 feet (60 cm) and spreading 18 inches (45 cm). It makes a valuable addition to the cool climate garden. From late summer to winter, the bleeding heart dies down completely. During early spring, tall, arching stems shoot out of the ground displaying many beautiful, ferny leaves. Once established, the delicate blooms promptly follow. ✿ **PLANTING** Choose a semishaded position in the perennial border for best results. Ideally, the soil should be rich, moist, and well-drained. Impoverished soils can be enriched prior to planting, with high-quality compost. Divisions are best replanted carefully during winter, and potted specimens planted in spring. ✿ **FLOWERING** Dainty blooms appear from late spring to early summer, after which the plant goes dormant. ✿ **CULTIVATION** Bleeding hearts are not at all tolerant of hot, dry conditions. Keep thoroughly moist and out of direct sunlight, otherwise death is inevitable. Mulch well and each spring supplement with a generous application of compost. Divide clumps every four years to prevent overcrowding. ✿ **PROPAGATION** By division in late winter or by stratified seed in autumn.

Digitalis grandiflora

Foxglove ◑ ● ❖❖❖

✿ **OTHER NAME** Yellow foxglove ✿ **DESCRIPTION** Honey-painted, tubular flowers with deep brown, mottled throats, make this foxglove so appealing. Apart from the colour, *Digitalis grandiflora* is identical in shape to its better known mauve cousins. It grows to a height of 2–3 feet (60–90 cm) and is unbranched in its habit. A rosette of smooth but strongly veined, lance-shaped leaves forms at the base, in much the same way as a dandelion. Cottage-style garden plants blend well with this captivating, short-lived perennial. After flowering, small rounded capsules release an abundance of seed.

✿ **PLANTING** Choose a protected, semishaded position with rich, moist, and well-drained soil. Seed can be sown direct, or young plants established during early spring. ✿ **FLOWERING** Flowers appear during early summer and may continue until midsummer. ✿ **CULTIVATION** Before the first set of blooms go to seed, remove them to ensure a second flush. After two or three years, extract the mature plants from the ground. The self-seeded plants will rapidly replace them. Keep moist throughout summer and feed regularly during the growing season with a balanced liquid fertilizer.

✿ **PROPAGATION** Seeds sown from mid- to late spring will produce blooms the following summer. Otherwise, clumps can be divided during autumn or spring.

Epimedium grandiflorum

Bishop's hat ❂ ❖❖❖

❀ **OTHER NAME** Longspur epimedium

❀ **DESCRIPTION** *Epimedium grandiflorum* is primarily valued for its delicate appearance, but tough, leathery heart-shaped foliage. In spring, the leaves are light green with noticeable pink veins. By midsummer, they become dark green and glossy in appearance, while reddish-bronze tones dominate in autumn. The dense, carpeting nature of this perennial plant makes it an excellent weed suppressor. This effect is enhanced with mass plantings. *Epimedium grandiflorum* grows to 1 foot (30 cm), spreading equally. The blooms are numerous and attractive in an unusual combination of red, white, and mauve. ❀ **PLANTING** *Epimediums* grow best in cool climate gardens, preferring light shade, protection from wind, and moist, compost-enriched soil. During early spring, position young plants 10 inches (25 cm) apart. ❀ **FLOWERING** A mass of flowers appear from late spring to early summer which are excellent for indoor vase arrangements.

❀ **CULTIVATION** Established clumps may be left undisturbed, except for the purpose of propagation. Keep moist throughout summer and apply slow-release fertilizer annually. Cut back prior to the new flush of growth in earliest spring and mulch generously with compost or leaf litter to keep the soil humus-rich. ❀ **PROPAGATION** Divide established clumps in spring or autumn and replant immediately.

Euphorbia polychroma (syn. *Euphorbia epithymoides*)
Cushion euphorbia ◑ ❖❖❖

✿ **OTHER NAME** Spurge ✿ **DESCRIPTION** This is a delightful perennial for the cool climate rock garden or perennial border. Like all members of the Euphorbia family, however, its milky sap contains irritants that can affect people with sensitive skins. For this reason, it is advisable to wear gloves when pruning or handling the plant. *Euphorbia polychroma* has a naturally rounded shape and an attractive, bushy appearance. It grows 20 inches (50 cm) high with a similar spread. In late spring, stunning yellow bracts contrast beautifully with the mid-green foliage beneath. The actual flowers are quite inconspicuous. They are yellowish-green and develop in loose, flattened clusters inside the bracts. During autumn, the leaves develop reddish tones. ✿ **PLANTING** Set young plants at 24 inch (60 cm) intervals during early spring. Euphorbias thrive in full sun but grow equally well in semi-shaded positions. Virtually any kind of soil is suitable, so long as it is well-drained. ✿ **FLOWERING** Brightly coloured bracts appear during spring, lasting several weeks. ✿ **CULTIVATION** *Euphorbia polychroma* demands little attention and pests or diseases are rarely a problem. Keep the soil moist throughout the hottest months and drier during winter. Occasional applications of liquid fertilizer during the growing season will aid flower development. ✿ **PROPAGATION** By seed sown in spring or cuttings.

Geranium maculatum
American cranesbill ⊘ pH ❖❖❖

✿ **DESCRIPTION** *Geranium maculatum* is a useful perennial species, due to its ability to thrive in waterlogged soils. In its natural habitat, the American cranesbill can be found growing in swamps and damp woodland areas. From a stout rootstock, graceful 20–28 inch (50–70 cm) hairy, unbranched stems emerge, which bear pale pink, upward-facing, saucer-shaped blooms in spring; often with white centres. A pure-white variety also exists known as *Geranium maculatum* 'Album'. During autumn, tiny black seeds develop that are ejected from the plant. The leaves are sparse, deeply divided, with toothed edges.
✿ **PLANTING** A protected and semi-shaded position is best with moist, slightly acidic, humus-rich soil. New plants can be established in early spring and spaced 20 inches (50 cm) apart. ✿ **FLOWERING** Blooms appear from late spring through to midsummer. ✿ **CULTIVATION** Prune after flowering to induce a flush of new growth. Top-dress the surrounding soil each spring with leaf litter to provide a steady flow of nutrients throughout the year. Mulching is also advisable. Once established, the American cranesbill will naturalize happily under large trees and shrubs. Sometimes they may become affected by rust. ✿ **PROPAGATION** By seed sown in autumn, division in autumn, or basal cuttings taken in early spring.

Helleborus orientalis

Lenten rose ◑ ● p̂H ❖❖❖

❀ **DESCRIPTION** Once established, you can always rely on the delightful lenten rose to provide a splash of interest at the end of a dreary winter. This cool-climate perennial bears numerous solitary, cup-shaped, and downward-facing blooms in varying shades of purple and green. Lenten roses grow to 18 inches (45 cm), spreading equally, and multiply at a speedy pace in ideal conditions. Large, divided, glossy leaves provide interest all year round but should be guarded against damaging slugs and snails. ❀ **PLANTING** Lenten roses prefer rich, moist, and well-drained soil with a neutral to alkaline pH. They thrive in the shade and make loving companions for large trees and shrubs. Enrich the soil with generous quantities of compost prior to planting. Sow fresh seed or plant out new specimens during spring and keep moist. ❀ **FLOWERING** Flowers appear from late winter to late spring, lasting several months. ❀ **CULTIVATION** Water regularly throughout summer and watch for aphid attacks. If you like, trim the leaves back before flowering. Enrich the soil annually with an organic mulch and avoid disturbing the plants once settled. ❀ **PROPAGATION** Sow fresh seed in spring or divide established clumps in autumn. Be mindful that the roots are poisonous.

Hepatica nobilis (syn. *Anemone hepatica*)

Hepatica ◑ pH ❖❖❖

✿ **DESCRIPTION** A delightful little semi-evergreen, dome-shaped
perennial for shady situations. It grows to a height of 6 inches (15 cm) and
produces dainty, pale pink to purple or white, cup-shaped blooms in spring.
The leaves are rounded, deeply and acutely lobed, sometimes tinged with
purple beneath. Hepaticas are well-suited to woodland gardens and choice
rockery positions where they do not have to compete with vigorous neighbours.
They are semi-evergreen in all but the coldest areas and thrive in pots when
grown in cool greenhouse conditions. ✿ **PLANTING** Deep, moist, humus-
rich soil is essential, with a pH of 5.5–6.5. Build up garden beds prior to
planting with leaf litter or well-rotted compost. Establish in spring, spacing
plants 6 inches (15 cm) apart. ✿ **FLOWERING** Blooms appear from early
spring and continue for several weeks. ✿ **CULTIVATION** The stout,
branched roots resent disturbance and are slow to re-establish. Keep moist,
particularly through summer, and mulch well to retain soil moisture.
Flowering is improved with annual dressings of compost and slow-release
fertilizer during late spring. Pests and diseases are rarely a problem.
✿ **PROPAGATION** By fresh seed sown in early summer or division in
late spring or autumn.

Heuchera sanguinea
Coral bells ◔ ❖❖❖

❀ **DESCRIPTION** *Heuchera sanguinea* is often found in an old, established garden. It is not commonly seen today, but is nevertheless a very useful plant for mass display, perennial borders, and narrow garden beds. Its foliage is soft and geranium-like, and the young leaves are brushed with attractive, coppery tones. Coral bells are evergreen perennials and eventually form large clumps. From late spring to early autumn, dainty, nodding flowers are borne on tall, wiry stems from 1 to 2 feet (30 to 60 cm) high. A number of varieties are available that range in colour from fiery red to the purest of whites. Traditionally, however, the flowers are coral pink. ❀ **PLANTING** Select a partially shaded position with light, moist, well-drained soil. Young plants will greatly benefit if the soil is supplemented with organic matter prior to planting. Set plants 1 foot (30 cm) apart during spring. ❀ **FLOWERING** Flowers do not develop until the plant is two years old, but once established they appear from late spring to early autumn. ❀ **CULTIVATION** Divide clumps every five years during autumn to prevent overcrowding, and remove blooms as they fade. Keep moist throughout summer and feed annually. ❀ **PROPAGATION** By seed or division in autumn.

Hosta fortunei
Fortune's plantain lily ◑ ● ✦✦✦

✿ **DESCRIPTION** *Hosta fortunei* is a vigorous, clump-forming perennial that thrives in all but the coldest climates. It produces large, luxurious, dark green leaves, which are grey-green in colour and heavily veined. Pale lilac, funnel-shaped flowers emerge in summer in loose clusters, but are not particularly notable. *Hostas* provide a useful backdrop to other perennial plants and are often grown near poolsides or along the banks of streams. The foliage reaches 2–3 feet (60–90 cm) in height, dies back during winter, and reemerges the following spring. ✿ **PLANTING** Choose a protected and shaded position with rich, moist, well-drained soil. Add generous amounts of leaf litter and compost, and space plants 24 inches (60 cm) apart. Early spring is the best time to plant. ✿ **FLOWERING** Blooms appear throughout summer and last for several weeks. ✿ **CULTIVATION** Protect new growth in spring from marauding snails and slugs, otherwise the foliage can be badly damaged. Keep moist throughout the growing season, and feed lavishly with compost and manure in spring to give the plants a flying start. Remove flowers as they fade and the foliage once it has completely withered. Clumps may remain undisturbed indefinitely, except for the purpose of propagation. ✿ **PROPAGATION** Divide established clumps in early spring.

Kirengeshoma palmata

Kirengeshoma ◐ pH ❖❖❖

❁ **DESCRIPTION** An unusual but charming upright perennial herb that is a native of Japan and grows well in shaded areas of the garden if the right soil conditions are provided. Growing to 4 feet (1.2 m) in height it has slender dark stems and attractive rounded, lobed foliage that is mid-green in colour. The nodding, bell-shaped flowers are borne in sprays held above the foliage. They are small and creamy yellow. ❁ **PLANTING** To grow successfully, the soil must be rich and moist with plenty of well-rotted leaf litter added. Prepare the ground well prior to planting, and keep well watered until plants are established. ❁ **FLOWERING** From late summer to autumn. ❁ **CULTIVATION** Water frequently in spring and summer, especially if conditions are hot and dry. Mulch around the base of the plants with leaf mulch to keep weed growth down and prevent the soil from drying out. ❁ **PROPAGATION** Either by seed, which should be sown in spring, or by division of clumps in autumn or spring.

Lamium galeobdolon (syn. *Lamiastrum galeobdolon*)

Yellow archangel ◑ ● ❖❖❖

✿ **OTHER NAME** Golden dead nettle ✿ **DESCRIPTION** This semi-evergreen, creeping perennial is an extremely prolific grower and thrives under the shade of large trees or shrubs. Yellow archangels grow to a height of 1 foot (30 cm) and will spread invasively if permitted. Indeed, gardeners must be vigilant in preventing this eager ground cover from taking over the entire garden. It has strong, creeping runners that are hollow and quadrangular in shape. They produce mid-green, sharply pointed, oval leaves. From late spring to early summer, yellow archangels display a mass of lemon-yellow, tubular flowers. They are bi-lipped and occur in whorls.
✿ **PLANTING** Find a protected position where nothing seems to grow, and it will be just fine for this little plant. Yellow archangels will tolerate partial or full shade but prefer moist, well-drained soils. Ensure that there is ample room for growth. Steep slopes and difficult-to-weed areas are ideal locations. Plant during spring or autumn, spacing young plants at 2–3 feet (60–90 cm) intervals or more. ✿ **FLOWERING** Blooms from late spring to early summer. ✿ **CULTIVATION** Keep soil moist throughout summer and apply a little complete fertilizer during spring. Remove over-adventurous runners. ✿ **PROPAGATION** By seed or division of runners in winter.

Liriope muscari
Lilyturf ◑ ● ❖❖❖

❀ **OTHER NAME** Big blue lilyturf ❀ **DESCRIPTION** *Liriope muscari* is an enchanting evergreen perennial, which grows from an enlarged, fleshy rhizome. From late summer to autumn, it has dense spikes of deep purple, bell-shaped blooms against a background of dark green, strappy leaves. Flowers are promptly followed by tiny black berries in late autumn. A highly attractive variegated form is also available. Lilyturfs grow to 1 foot (30 cm), spreading half as much again. Their compact size and shape makes them ideal for border edging or for planting along pathways. They thrive in a wide range of light conditions, but growth is slow in heavily shaded areas.
❀ **PLANTING** Choose a protected and partially shaded position with rich, moist, and well-drained soil. Plant in spring, spacing them at a distance of 1 foot (30 cm), and water well afterwards to settle the roots.
❀ **FLOWERING** Flowers appear from late summer to early autumn followed by a mass of small berries. ❀ **CULTIVATION** In early spring, remove the older leaves to encourage a flush of new growth. Organic fertilizer can also be applied at this time. Keep lilyturfs moist throughout the growing season and mulch well to preserve soil moisture.
❀ **PROPAGATION** Divide and replant clumps in early spring or sow fresh seed in autumn.

Lobelia syphilitica
Big blue lobelia ❂ ❖❖❖

✿ **DESCRIPTION** *Lobelia syphilitica* is a useful plant for poolsides and informal gardens and is able to flourish in heavy, damp soil. From late summer to autumn, it reveals a welcome splash of blue by way of pretty, bi-lipped blooms. When the floral display is over, tiny seeds spread freely throughout the garden, which germinate the following spring. The complementary leaves are small, narrow, and oval in shape. *Lobelia syphilitica* is a narrow, clump-forming perennial, and usually grows to a height of 3 feet 4 inches (1 m).
✿ **PLANTING** Partially shaded positions are preferred, with moist, well-drained soil. This lobelia will tolerate dampness during hot weather but detests 'wet feet' in winter, so good drainage is important. Establish plants in small groups for a really decorative effect. ✿ **CULTIVATION** Prune after flowering and keep moist throughout summer. Each spring, feed the soil with composted manure and mulch well, particularly if the soil has a tendency to dry out. Regular applications of liquid fertilizer during summer will also be beneficial. ✿ **PROPAGATION** Established plants may be lifted and divided during autumn or early spring. Do not allow the roots to dry out during this process. Fresh seed may also be sown at these times.

Lysimachia nummularia

Creeping Jenny ◑ ❖❖❖

❀ **OTHER NAME** Moneywort ❀ **DESCRIPTION** A popular and easy-to-grow perennial ground cover reaching 1–2 inches (2.5–5 cm) in height that spreads rapidly by runners. It is a useful weed suppressor and thrives in wet, shaded areas where many other plants will not grow. It is hardy and easily recognized by its coin-like, mid-green leaves and bright yellow blossoms. It is suitable for growing on banks, between stepping stones, or over terraced walls. *Lysimachia nummularia* 'Aurea' is an attractive, golden-leaved variety that is often grown near garden ponds.
❀ **PLANTING** Plant runners at any time into rich, moist soil in a shady position. Loosen the topsoil beforehand and space the runners at 1–1½ feet (30–45 cm) intervals to form a thick mat. Do not allow the young plants to dry out. ❀ **FLOWERING** Flowers profusely throughout summer.
❀ **CULTIVATION** In the right situation, very little maintenance is required. It does not tolerate drought, so keep it well watered throughout summer. Mulch generously around the plants to preserve the moisture in the soil. Unwanted runners are easily pulled out if they spread too far. Feed during spring with a complete fertilizer. ❀ **PROPAGATION** Transplant runners at any time.

Maranta leuconeura var. *Kerchoviana*
Rabbit tracks ◑ ❖

❀ **OTHER NAME** Herringbone plant ❀ **DESCRIPTION** *Marantas*
are among the most spectacular of all foliage plants and this variety is
certainly no exception. Its large green oblong leaves have fascinating deep
green markings that resemble the footprints of rabbits, hence the common
name. They also have a very interesting response to light. By day, the leaves
open out flat, and at night, they curl upright. It is an evergreen perennial
and grows to a height of 12 inches (30 cm) at best, spreading equally. In
cool and temperate regions, these plants must be grown under glass or
indoors, as they do not tolerate frost. The potted plants are suitable to be
moved into shady areas of the garden in summer. High humidity is also
essential for their growth. ❀ **PLANTING** Outdoors, they thrive in moist,
humus-rich soil in protected, shaded positions. Houseplant specimens
should be grown in squat pots containing high-quality potting mix, and
placed in bright, indirect light. ❀ **FLOWERING** Insignificant single
white flowers are produced during summer but are best removed.
❀ **CULTIVATION** Keep the soil moist throughout the growing season
and on the dry side over winter. Container plants should be repotted
annually, and fed with liquid fertilizer every two months over spring and
summer. Remove dried or damaged leaves anytime, and divide clumps every
third year. ❀ **PROPAGATION** By stem cuttings in summer or division in
spring and summer.

Meconopsis cambrica
Welsh poppy ◑ pH ❖❖❖

✿ **DESCRIPTION** Close relatives of the Welsh poppy have a reputation for being difficult to grow, but the Welsh variety will grow happily in any cool or temperate region. It is a spreading perennial that grows 12–18 inches (30–45 cm) high and produces bright lemon or orange blooms on tall, narrow stems. Heavily petalled double forms are also available. The soft, divided, fern-like leaves develop in rosettes and provide a complementary backdrop. Plant en masse for a spectacular display. ✿ **PLANTING** The soil should be moist and humus-rich with a pH of 5.5–6.5. Good drainage is also important, particularly during winter. Choose a sheltered, partially shaded position and either sow seed directly or space young plants from 12 to 15 inches (30 to 38 cm) apart. ✿ **FLOWERING** From late spring to early summer. ✿ **CULTIVATION** Divide clumps every three years to maintain vigour, and remove spent blooms. Supplement the soil annually with compost or leaf litter. If your Welsh poppies are to survive, it is important to keep them moist throughout the growing season and drier over winter. ✿ **PROPAGATION** Sow fresh seed in late summer or divide clumps in early spring. Double forms can only be propagated by division.

Mertensia virginica (syn. *Mertensia pulmonarioides*)
Virginia bluebell ◐ ❖❖❖

❀ **DESCRIPTION** This elegant perennial bears clusters of deep blue nodding tubular blooms in spring which emerge on tall spikes. Its soft green oval leaves are stemless and wrap around the main flowering stem where they join. They grow 12–24 inches (30–60 cm) tall, spreading equally, but unlike many other perennials, the foliage begins to die down in late summer. Virginia bluebells thrive when grown amongst other plants and enjoy cool, woodland conditions in the shade of tall, deciduous trees. ❀ **PLANTING** Choose a protected, semi-shaded position with moist, well-drained soil. During spring, plant young specimens 12 inches (30 cm) apart. Do not allow the soil to dry out during the establishment phase. ❀ **FLOWERING** Blooms appear throughout spring and last for several weeks. ❀ **CULTIVATION** Virginia bluebells flourish in cool to temperate climates and are tolerant of frost, but they are unable to survive hot, dry conditions. Water generously during the growing season and feed in spring with a good dose of complete fertilizer. Snails and slugs favour the crowns, therefore some form of protection is necessary. An organic mulch will keep the roots cool and moist and help to suppress weed growth. ❀ **PROPAGATION** By seed sown in autumn or division in spring or autumn.

Myosotis scorpioides
Water forget-me-not ◑ ❖❖❖

❀ **DESCRIPTION** The name forget-me-not is very appropriate for this delightful plant which returns faithfully year after year. The water forget-me-not is a deciduous to semi-evergreen perennial that grows as a marginal plant by poolsides, streams, or in boggy areas of the garden. The smooth, narrow leaves form loose mounds reaching 6-12 inches (15-30 cm) in height. During late spring and summer, a profusion of cobalt-blue flowers appear with tiny, yellow centres. These are promptly followed by glossy black seeds that spread freely throughout the garden. ❀ **PLANTING** Plant seedlings during early spring at 1 foot (30 cm) intervals. The soil should be boggy or marshy for best results, and the site must be protected from strong winds and the harsh afternoon sun. Prior to planting, incorporate some compost and manure into the surrounding soil. ❀ **FLOWERING** From late spring to summer. ❀ **CULTIVATION** Water forget-me-nots are not at all tolerant of dry conditions and must be kept moist at all times. Annual dressings of well-rotted manure during spring will encourage prolific flowering and lush foliage growth. Remove the spent flowers if you do not wish them to self-seed, otherwise lightly trim during autumn once the seeds have dispersed. ❀ **PROPAGATION** By seed sown in autumn.

Polemonium caeruleum

Jacob's ladder ☽ ❖❖❖

✿ **DESCRIPTION** An exquisite clump-forming perennial for the cool, woodland garden is *Polemonium caeruleum*, better known as Jacob's ladder. It carries delightful panicles of mauve cup-shaped blossoms throughout spring and summer, sometimes with white and yellow centres. Jacob's ladder achieves a height and spread of 20–24 inches (50–60 cm) and sends up mounds of feathery, apple-green leaves in early spring. Blue and white forms are also available. ✿ **PLANTING** During early spring, plant in light shade and moist, well-drained soil that has been previously enriched with compost or leaf litter. Space 18 inches (45 cm) apart. ✿ **FLOWERING** Blooms appear from late spring to midsummer. ✿ **CULTIVATION** If the soil dries out, the foliage rapidly deteriorates, so keep moist and mulch heavily to prevent this from occurring. Spent flowers should be removed in autumn when they have faded. In early spring, prune the entire plant back hard to induce a new flush of growth. These fibrous-rooted plants are gross feeders and rapidly deplete the soil of nutrients. For this reason, feed generously each spring with a complete fertilizer and supplement the soil with monthly applications of liquid manure. ✿ **PROPAGATION** Established clumps are best divided in autumn or early spring. Sow fresh seed in autumn.

Polygonatum multiflorum

Solomon's seal ◑ ❖❖❖

❀ **OTHER NAME** Eurasian Solomon's seal ❀ **DESCRIPTION**
Solomon's seal is a tall, leafy, arching perennial that grows best in temperate
climates. It produces sweetly scented white and green-tipped tubular
blooms in clusters of two to six, from the upper leaf axils. Bumble bees find
them particularly attractive. Solomon's seal normally reaches 3 feet 4 inches
(1 m) in height, but only spreads half this distance. Its leaves are large,
smooth, and oval in shape and die back in winter during the dormant
period. These hardy plants shoot from a large, fleshy, underground rhizome
and thrive in shaded perennial borders amongst other woodland plants.
Seed is set in early autumn. ❀ **PLANTING** Solomon's seal needs moist,
well-drained soil and thrives in partial shade. Sunny positions can be
tolerated, so long as the roots are shaded. Plant during early spring at 2 feet
(60 cm) intervals. ❀ **FLOWERING** Blooms appear from late spring to
early summer. ❀ **CULTIVATION** Keep moist throughout summer and
mulch well. Top-dress the surrounding soil annually in spring with compost
and manure. Prune back hard in autumn and watch out for sawfly
caterpillars in early summer. ❀ **PROPAGATION** Clumps may be divided
in autumn or early spring. Ripened seed sown in autumn will take several
years to flower.

peren, evergrn   6~9"

Polygonum affine (syn. *Persicaria affinis*)
Knotweed ○ ◑ ● ❖❖❖

❀ **OTHER NAME** Himalayan fleeceflower ❀ **DESCRIPTION** A useful, mat-forming evergreen perennial that can be grown as a quick-spreading ground cover in a wide range of soils and climates. Knotweed grows from 6 to 9 inches (15 to 30 cm) in height, with stout stems that carry small, glossy green, lance-shaped leaves that turn bronze during winter. The flowers appear in dense spikes and are small, funnel-shaped and rosy red. Varieties include 'Darjeeling Red', which has deep red flower spikes, and 'Donald Lowndes', which has red flowers that fade to pink. Suitable for shady parts of the garden, it is ideal for the rockery or as a vigorous ground cover to bind together a steeply sloping bank. ❀ **PLANTING** Knotweed can be grown in sun or shade in any moderately fertile garden soil, although damp soil will produce the best results. Water well until established, and mulch to help maintain soil moisture. ❀ **FLOWERING** Late summer and early autumn. ❀ **CULTIVATION** Additional water may be required during hot, dry spells. Take care that knotweed doesn't become too invasive, especially in garden beds where other species are being grown. ❀ **PROPAGATION** By seed in autumn, or by division during autumn or spring.

Potentilla x *tonguei*

Tormentilla cinquefoil ◕ ❖❖❖

❀ **DESCRIPTION** A compact, loose-forming perennial for the cottage garden or colourful perennial border. Growing to a height of 8 inches (20 cm), tormentilla cinquefoils have delightful, saucer-shaped, apricot blooms with contrasting, carmine-red centres. The narrow, dark green leaves are oval in shape and emerge from non-rooting stems that lay upon the ground. While these charming plants will be more prolific in sunny positions, the strong apricot hue is prone to fading. During autumn, small dry fruit develops where the flowers were. Known as achenes, each contains a solitary seed. ❀ **PLANTING** Grow in moderately rich, well-drained soil in light shade. A neutral pH is ideal. If the loam is too rich, lush foliage may be produced at the expense of the flowers. Best planting times are early summer and autumn. ❀ **FLOWERING** Long-lasting blooms occur in abundance from early summer to autumn. ❀ **CULTIVATION** Feed early in summer with a light dressing of complete fertilizer. Keep moist throughout the growing season and mulch well to prevent the soil from drying out. Prune in early spring, removing weak growth back to ground level. Stronger growth can be reduced by a third to encourage bushiness. ❀ **PROPAGATION** By softwood cuttings in summer. Seeds may be sown in autumn, but rarely grow true to type from cultivars.

Primula auricula

Auricula primrose   ◑ pH ❖❖❖

✿ **DESCRIPTION** The auricula primrose is easy to grow in temperate regions and is certainly one of the most delightful of all the alpine primroses. It is a clump-forming perennial that produces umbels of sweetly scented, yellow, flattened blooms. Single or double cultivars are also available in a variety of shades including white, purple, dark red, and blue. Attractive varieties include 'Hazel's Little White' which has showy, single white blooms. The leaves are soft, oval, and grey-green. Auricula primroses grow 6–10 inches (15–25 cm) in height, spreading equally. Their rounded habit makes them ideal companions for rockery plants. ✿ **PLANTING** Choose a partially shaded position with moist, acidic, fertile soil. A cool, moist root run is essential and is easily provided in a rockery situation. Establish new plants during early spring, spacing them from 6 to 12 inches (15 to 30 cm) apart. ✿ **FLOWERING** A procession of flowers appear from early to late spring. ✿ **CULTIVATION** Plants should never be allowed to dry out as they are not at all tolerant of drought. Mulch well to preserve soil moisture and feed regularly throughout spring and summer with liquid fertilizer. Remove flowers as they fade and replace older plants as they lose their vigour. ✿ **PROPAGATION** By ripened seed sown in summer or division of offsets in early autumn or spring.

Ramonda myconi
Rosette mullein ◑ pH ❖❖❖

✿ **DESCRIPTION** *Ramonda myconi* closely resembles its relative, the African violet in terms of its size and overall appearance. It is an evergreen perennial that produces small clusters of mauve, pink, or white flattened flowers in late spring. The leaves are hairy and wrinkled, with serrated margins. As with the African violet, they develop in rosettes. The entire plant is quite petite, growing to a mere 3 inches (7.5 cm). Good drainage is essential if they are to survive. For this reason, shaded rockeries and retaining walls are ideal locations to plant. *R. myconi* will also thrive in squat pots when placed in a cool, shaded position. ✿ **PLANTING** Prior to planting, condition the soil with dolomite lime, leaf litter, and sand should the drainage need improving. The position should receive early morning sun and be protected from strong winds. Young plants are best established in early spring and planted 4 inches (10 cm) apart. ✿ **FLOWERING** Dainty blooms appear from late spring to early summer. ✿ **CULTIVATION** Keep moist, particularly during summer, but avoid overwatering. Remove flowers as they fade and any damaged or diseased leaves. Feed monthly with liquid fertilizer. ✿ **PROPAGATION** By leaf cuttings or seed in early autumn, or by offsets in summer.

Sanguinaria canadensis

Bloodroot ◐ ❖❖❖

❀ **DESCRIPTION** The bloodroot is so named because of its fleshy, rhizomatous roots, which exude bright red sap when cut. It is a perennial from North America and is able to thrive in the driest of conditions, despite its delicate appearance. The waxy flowers are rather unique with their brilliant-white irregular-sized petals, arranged in two or more whorls, and contrasting golden stamens. Occasionally, the petals are tinged with pink or grey tones on the underside. The variety 'Multiplex' (syn. 'Flore pleno') has double flowers, also in pure-white. The slender stems are virtually naked and carry only one grey-green heart- or kidney-shaped leaf. After flowering, narrow, oblong seed pods develop. The plant's compact size of 4–6 inches (10–15 cm) makes it ideal for rockeries or gravelly slopes. ❀ **PLANTING** Bloodroots thrive in dry, rocky soils in partial shade. Good drainage is essential. Plant during early spring. ❀ **FLOWERING** Pure-white, waxy blooms emerge in spring followed by 1 inch (2.5 cm) seed pods. ❀ **CULTIVATION** Avoid overwatering at all costs and go easy on the fertilizers too. Occasional watering and applications of liquid fertilizer during the growing season are all that is required. Remove flowers as they fade. ❀ **PROPAGATION** Sow fresh seed in autumn or cleanly divide rhizomes in summer.

Streptocarpus saxorum

False African violet ◑ ❖

❀ **DESCRIPTION** *Streptocarpus saxorum* is a short-lived, tender perennial that originates from South Africa. Being frost and drought tender, it is best planted in a greenhouse during the winter in cold climates and potted plants can be moved to a shady area outdoors for a summer display. It is also readily sold as a houseplant. Under favourable conditions, it bears solitary, trumpet-shaped, lavender flowers upon upward-curling, wiry stems, over a long period. The small, succulent, grey-green leaves are velvety to the touch and have inrolled margins. When young, the stems are soft and pliable, becoming woody with age. Their trailing habit makes them ideal for use in hanging baskets, where the blooms can be observed at eye level. At maturity, false African violets reach 12 inches (30 cm) in height, with a spread of 8 inches (20 cm). ❀ **PLANTING** Plant during spring into light, well-drained soil. A position with bright, filtered light is preferred. However, the tender leaves should be protected from direct sun. ❀ **FLOWERING** Flowers appear from spring through to autumn. ❀ **CULTIVATION** Keep moist but not wet, and feed monthly during the growing season with half-strength liquid fertilizer. After flowering, remove the old spikes immediately, checking at the same time for any torn or diseased leaves. ❀ **PROPAGATION** By seed or leaf cuttings in summer.

Tellima grandiflora
Alaska fringecup ◑ ❖❖❖

✿ **DESCRIPTION** *Tellima grandiflora* is an effective ground-covering plant that looks most attractive when grown in shady rockeries. It is an evergreen, clump-forming perennial, and grows 2 feet (60 cm) in height. Right throughout the year its heart-shaped, apple green and purple-tinged leaves provide interest. They are lightly toothed and hairy to the touch. A purple-leaved variety, known as *T. grandiflora* 'Purpurea', is also available and contrasts beautifully with the original form. Small, creamy flowers are borne in late spring, which are fringed and bell-shaped. These are supported on upright spikes and held well above the foliage. Flowers on the purple-leaved variety are attractively tinged with pink. ✿ **PLANTING** Cool, lightly shaded woodland conditions are best, but the Alaska fringecup will also thrive in sunny borders when grown amongst other perennial shrubs. Most soils are suitable, so long as they are well-drained. Plant during spring, spacing new specimens 2 feet (60 cm) apart. ✿ **FLOWERING** In late spring, bell-shaped blooms appear, lasting two to three weeks.

✿ **CULTIVATION** Keep moist throughout summer and feed each spring with a complete fertilizer. Prune lightly after flowering, to maintain bushiness. Alaska fringecups are relatively pest- and disease-free.

✿ **PROPAGATION** Divide established clumps in spring or sow seed in autumn.

Tradescantia fluminensis (syn. *Tradescantia albiflora*)

Wandering Jew ◑ ❖❖

♣ **DESCRIPTION** Around the world these plants are favoured as houseplants but grow equally well outdoors in cool, shaded gardens where their rooting stems spread rapidly. These evergreen perennials are prized for their semi-succulent, glossy, pale green leaves, often tinged with purple beneath. The two-toned effect and trailing habit make the Wandering Jew a terrific hanging basket specimen. A most attractive, variegated form is also available with creamy-white stripes. Intermittently, tiny clusters of white blooms appear throughout spring and summer. Wandering Jews grow 2 inches (5 cm) high and trail 2 feet (60 cm) or more when cultivated in a pot. Outdoors, they spread indefinitely. ♣ **PLANTING** Container specimens should be planted in a quality potting mix and placed in a position that receives bright but filtered sunlight. In the garden, choose a partially shaded position with moist, well-drained soil. Plant during spring. ♣ **FLOWERING** Blooms periodically throughout the growing season. ♣ **CULTIVATION** Repot container plants every spring and pinch the foliage back regularly to promote bushiness. Slow-release fertilizer pellets will provide all the nutrients necessary. Ensure that outdoor plants do not get out of hand by ripping out unwanted rooting stems. Keep moist but do not overwater. ♣ **PROPAGATION** By stem cuttings taken any time of year.

Trillium grandiflorum
Snow trillium ◑ ● pH ❖❖❖

❀ **OTHER NAME** White wake robin ❀ **DESCRIPTION** *Trillium grandiflorum* is an enchanting perennial for the cool climate, woodland garden. It has captivating, three-petalled blooms that open white and later change to pink, framed by a whorl of three dark green, strategically placed leaves. *T. grandiflorum* grows from a short, underground rhizome and reaches a height of 16–20 inches (40–50 cm). ❀ **PLANTING** During late summer, plant rhizomes 6 inches (15 cm) apart at a depth of 4 inches (10 cm), in rich, well-drained, neutral to acid soil. The addition of leaf litter or compost at planting time will improve the soil's water-holding capacity and help to lower the pH. They enjoy dappled shade, in a cool, protected part of the garden. ❀ **FLOWERING** During spring its delightful blooms create a vivid display over several weeks. ❀ **CULTIVATION** Keep moist throughout the growing season and feed annually with a dressing of well-rotted compost and manure. A protective layer of mulch is advisable in areas with severe winter conditions. Dead-head spent blooms immediately, but do not remove the stems and leaves until they have died back completely. ❀ **PROPAGATION** Divide and replant rhizomes in late summer or sow seed into punnets during spring.

Tulbaghia violacea
Wild garlic ◑ ❖❖

✿ **OTHER NAME** Violet tulbaghia

✿ **DESCRIPTION** A charming clump-forming, bulbous-rooted perennial that makes a very pretty potted plant for a greenhouse or indoors in cool to cold climates. Growing to 2 feet (60 cm) in height, it forms a pleasant clump of slender, bright green foliage from which emerge tall stems topped by umbels of bright lilac-purple or pink flowers, which are very decorative. The flowers have a strong aroma, similar to that of garlic, hence its common name 'Wild garlic'. ✿ **PLANTING** To produce good results this plant must be provided with quite rich, moist but well-drained soil that has been fortified with plenty of organic matter in the form of well-rotted compost or manure prior to planting. ✿ **FLOWERING** The flowers appear in late spring and into summer. ✿ **CULTIVATION** Water routinely, especially during the main growing seasons of spring and summer. Reduce watering as the weather cools and the foliage begins to die back.

✿ **PROPAGATION** Either by division of clumps in spring or from seed sown in autumn or spring.

Uvularia perfoliata
Wood merrybells ◐ pH ❖❖❖

✿ **OTHER NAME** Bellwort ✿ **DESCRIPTION** For gardeners
interested in the unusual, *Uvularia perfoliata* is well worth a second glance.
This exquisite, clump-forming perennial thrives in woodland conditions, in
cool to temperate zones. During spring, enthralling clusters of pale yellow,
pendular blooms, beckon you into the garden. They are bell-shaped, with
intriguingly twisted petals. Looking very narcissistic, they hang gracefully
from upright, slender stems. The leaves are narrow and mid-green in colour.
They reach 1½ feet (45 cm) in height, spreading a conservative distance of
12 inches (30 cm). For best effect, establish several clumps together beneath
your favourite tree. ✿ **PLANTING** *U. perfoliata* enjoys moist, peaty,
woodland soils with a pH of 5.5–6.5. If your soil is not up to par, mix in a
little compost, peat, or acidic potting mix. Plant during autumn or spring at
12 inch (30 cm) spacings. ✿ **FLOWERING** Flowers appear in succession
throughout spring. ✿ **CULTIVATION** Do not apply inorganic fertilizers.
U. perfoliata requires a wholesome meal of leaf litter and compost once a
year. Keep moist at all times and remove blooms as they fade. Clumps
should remain undisturbed, except for the purposes of propagation.
✿ **PROPAGATION** By division in autumn or early spring.

Viola cornuta

Violet ◑ ❖❖❖

✿ **OTHER NAMES** Horned violet, Tufted pansy

✿ **DESCRIPTION** A charming little perennial ground cover for the shade garden is *Viola cornuta*, with attractive foliage and small mauve to purplish-blue spurred flowers in spring. Each bloom is flattened with the lower petal intriguingly angular in shape. Violets are semi-evergreen and creeping in habit, growing to a height of 12 inches (30 cm), with a spread of 8 inches (20 cm). This tufting plant produces dark green serrated leaves that emerge and spread from an underground rhizome. Cool to temperate climates are the most favourable for growth. ✿ **PLANTING** Choose a position with light shade and rich, moist soil. Beneath a deciduous tree is ideal. Before planting, enrich the area with compost and manure. Transplant divided clumps during winter, ensuring they do not dry out. In spring, set new plants 8 inches (20 cm) apart. ✿ **FLOWERING** A profusion of miniature blooms appears from late spring to summer. ✿ **CULTIVATION** Mulch well to prevent the soil from drying out, and water regularly throughout summer. A dose of complete fertilizer during spring is all the food they require. Thin out clumps every five years to renew their vigour and remove dried leaves in autumn. ✿ **PROPAGATION** Divide clumps in winter, and sow seed from mid to late summer.

Cardiocrinum giganteum
Giant lily ◑ pH ❖❖❖

❀ **DESCRIPTION** One of the most majestic of all flowering bulbs would be *Cardiocrinum giganteum*, better known as the giant lily. Both the botanical and common names however, allude to its flower size and indeed, the blooms are big and beautiful. Each leafy flowering stem produces a weighty 20 to 25 white, fragrant, trumpet-shaped blooms. They display decorative reddish-brown streaks inside. Dark green, heart-shaped leaves contrast beautifully with the flowers, and brown seed pods develop in autumn. The bulb itself is enormous. Giant lilies grow to 10 feet (3 m), spreading 30 inches (75 cm) or more. After flowering, the bulb dies and produces offsets. ❀ **PLANTING** During autumn, plant bulbs in a semishaded position with deep, moist, humus-rich soil. Dig a trench 20 inches (50 cm) deep, and line with leaf litter, compost, sand, and garden soil. Position bulbs with the neck facing upwards and bury so that each bulb lies just beneath the soil surface. Offsets take three to five years to flower. ❀ **FLOWERING** Blooms in summer, lasting for several weeks. ❀ **CULTIVATION** Keep bulbs well watered and mulched over summer. Feed during late summer when they begin to die back. ❀ **PROPAGATION** From bulblets planted in autumn or by seed in autumn or winter.

Clivia miniata
Scarlet kaffir lily ◖ ● ❖

❀ **DESCRIPTION** In warm to temperate climates, scarlet kaffir lilies provide a splash of colour in shady areas of the garden where many other plants refuse to flower. Their thick, fleshy roots produce arching, leathery, dark green leaves that grow outwards from the base, creating an attractive fan shape. Kaffir lilies are evergreen perennials and provide an element of interest all year round with their shapely appearance. Their strong stems, 16–18 inches (40–45 cm) high, carry a cluster of fragrant, orange or scarlet, bell-shaped blooms with yellow centres. These may appear at any time of year, but most prolifically in spring. In cool to cold climates, Kaffir lilies can be grown successfully in pots, then taken under glass in winter. ❀ **PLANTING** Plant bulbs from autumn to spring, in a shady area of the garden, with light, well-drained soil. ❀ **FLOWERING** Flowers appear during autumn and winter, but most dramatically in spring. ❀ **CULTIVATION** In cool climate areas, grow kaffir lilies either indoors or in greenhouse conditions to avoid frost damage. Water generously in summer and autumn, reducing considerably throughout winter. Watch for mealy bug infestations. ❀ **PROPAGATION** Sow seed in winter or spring, and divide clumps during spring or after flowering.

Convallaria majalis
Lily of the valley ◐ pH ❖❖❖

✿ **DESCRIPTION** This is one of the most popular fragrant bulbs for cool and temperate gardens. Lily of the valley bears clusters of delightful, small white, bell-shaped flowers that hang from a short, upright spike. For decades, the blooms have been popular for use in bridal bouquets and small vase arrangements. Also, each swollen rhizome pip produces an attractive pair of bright green, lance-shaped leaves, which die down over winter. Lily of the valley grows 8–12 inches (20–30 cm) tall and spreads by creeping rhizomes. Cold winters are essential for successful cultivation. ✿ **PLANTING** Establish pips at the end of autumn, burying them just below the soil surface. The soil should be light, well-drained, humus-rich, and slightly acidic in pH. Choose a protected position with morning sun or dappled shade.
✿ **FLOWERING** Flowers appear from late spring to early summer, lasting three to four weeks. ✿ **CULTIVATION** Mulch and manure bulbs generously in autumn and keep moist throughout the growing period. Remove flowers as they fade and the foliage after it has completely died back. Divide and replant congested pips every five years during late autumn. Plants are susceptible to grey mould. ✿ **PROPAGATION** During autumn, plant pips, or sow seed under glass.

Erythronium californicum

California fawn-lily ✿ pH ❖❖❖

✿ **DESCRIPTION** An exquisite spring-flowering bulb for the cool climate garden is the California fawn-lily. It grows in clumps from an underground tuber, is frost hardy, and has attractively mottled, glossy green leaves. As the weather warms, spectacular creamy-white flowers emerge with yellow centres and reflexing petals. Sometimes the outside petals are painted a complementary reddish-brown. California fawn-lilies grow 6–14 inches (15–35 cm) high, and spread 4–5 inches (10–12 cm).

✿ **PLANTING** Choose a partially shaded position with rich, loose, acidic soil. Prepare it well by incorporating generous quantities of compost and manure beforehand. Plant tubers 3 inches (7.5 cm) deep and 6 inches (15 cm) apart, anytime from summer to autumn. ✿ **FLOWERING** Up to three blooms appear on each flowering stem during spring, lasting several weeks. ✿ **CULTIVATION** The roots should never be allowed to dry out. For this reason, it is wise to mulch with peat, or leaf litter every two or three years in autumn. The tubers resent being transplanted and if possible, should remain undisturbed indefinitely. ✿ **PROPAGATION** Separate cormlets in summer or autumn and replant immediately to prevent dehydration. Seed sown in autumn will take five years to flower.

Galanthus nivalis
Snowdrop ◐ ❖❖❖

❀ **DESCRIPTION** Snowdrops are often the first spring flowering bulbs
to appear in the garden. Their enchanting white blooms are composed of three
green-tipped inner petals and three larger, unmarked petals. They produce
long, strap-like leaves which grow to a height of 3–8 inches (7.5–20 cm)
and are well suited to naturalizing under a canopy of deciduous trees.
Snowdrops are also suitable for planting in rockeries and on the edge of
shady, perennial borders. ❀ **PLANTING** Plant bulbs during autumn into
fertile, moist, and well-drained soil. Space them 4 to 6 inches (10 to 15 cm)
apart and provide a protected, partially shaded position. Snowdrops also do
well in pots, provided the soil is rich, friable, and kept moist throughout the
growing season. ❀ **FLOWERING** Flowering occurs from late winter to
early spring, for up to a month. ❀ **CULTIVATION** Protection from frost
is not necessary and bulbs can safely remain undisturbed in the ground for
several years. Keep moist throughout summer and remove the foliage after it
has thoroughly died back. If plants become congested, divide and replant
after flowering, ensuring that the bulbs do not dry out in the process. Watch
for nematode attacks. ❀ **PROPAGATION** By seed or bulblet division.

Hippeastrum hybrids

Hippeastrum   ◑ pH ❖

✿ **DESCRIPTION** Hippeastrums make a bold statement with their clusters of large open, trumpet-shaped flowers in shades of white, pink, red and salmon, and various combinations. Dark green clump-forming, strap-like leaves promptly follow the flowers, and in late summer, die back again. They grow 20–30 inches (50–75 cm) in height and thrive in temperate to warm zones. Hippeastrums are also very adaptable to pot culture and may be grown indoors or in greenhouse conditions in cooler climates and then moved outside to a shady part of the garden in summer.

✿ **PLANTING** Select a position with partial shade and rich, moist, well-drained acidic soil. Bury the bulbs with their necks above soil level from autumn to winter. Potted specimens require several hours of sunlight each day and a soil blend of equal parts peat, sand, leaf litter, and commercial potting mix. ✿ **FLOWERING** Breathtaking blooms appear from late winter to spring. ✿ **CULTIVATION** During dormancy, suspend bulbs in a cool, airy place to dry until the following autumn. When planted, water thoroughly only once, prior to the appearance of a flowering stem. From then on keep the soil moist and feed monthly with a liquid fertilizer until the leaves begin to wither. Protection from snails and slugs is essential.

✿ **PROPAGATION** By spring division of bulblets.

Hyacinthoides hispanica (syn. *Endymion hispanius*)
Spanish wood hyacinth ◐ ❖❖❖

❀ **OTHER NAME** Spanish bluebell ❀ **DESCRIPTION** Spanish wood hyacinths make a delightful addition to the shaded rockery or cottage garden. The clump-forming bulbs also naturalize freely under a canopy of deciduous trees and tall flowering shrubs. During spring, dense clusters of pendent, blue, bell-shaped blooms rise above a bed of glossy dark green ribbon-like leaves. Plants reach 12 inches (10–15 cm) in height and spread 4–6 inches (10–15 cm). In early summer, the leaves begin to wither, and the bulbs go into dormancy. They also thrive in pots and their blooms are particularly useful in cut flower arrangements. ❀ **PLANTING** During early autumn, establish bulbs in dappled shade 8 to 10 inches (20 to 25 cm) apart and 4 inches (10 cm) deep. Ideally, the soil should be heavy and moist. Potted bulbs are best placed in a cool, dark position for eight to ten weeks, before being brought out into the light. ❀ **FLOWERING** Flowers appear during early spring and bloom for several weeks. ❀ **CULTIVATION** Keep moist during active growth and drier over winter. Remove flowers as they fade and allow bulbs to remain undisturbed in the ground. Fertilizing is not necessary. ❀ **PROPAGATION** By seed in autumn or division of bulbs in late summer.

Ipheion uniflorum

Spring starflower ◑ ❖❖❖

❀ **DESCRIPTION** A charming group of small bulbs that can be grown in the shade with great success, creating a pretty display of starry flowers in early spring. Growing to 10 inches (15 cm) in height, its bulb generates a clump of slender pale green leaves that have a strange onion aroma if crushed. From the foliage emerge slender stems topped by delicate starry flowers in the pale to dark blue range. The variety 'Wisley blue' has particularly attractive deep blue blooms. ❀ **PLANTING** Dig the ground over well and incorporate some organic matter, then sow the bulbs in autumn to create a dense clump. The soil should be light and well-drained, yet still contain sufficient humus to retain moisture during summer. If drainage is a problem, create above-ground beds using plenty of extra compost, or consider using drainage pipes to take moisture away from the area. ❀ **FLOWERING** Blossoms from early spring. ❀ **CULTIVATION** Water routinely, taking care not to overwater as, like most bulbs, they resent very damp conditions. After flowering is finished and the foliage has begun to die back, feed with general purpose fertilizer and allow the foliage to completely wither and die. Reduce watering over summer. ❀ **PROPAGATION** By offsets in early autumn.

Iris cristata
Crested iris   ◑ ❖❖❖

✿ **DESCRIPTION** These delightful plants spread using creeping
rhizomes that move along the soil surface, and these should not be covered
with soil or they will rot. Growing to 4 inches (10 cm) in height, they are
small growing plants with neat fans of upright, lance-shaped foliage that dies
back in winter, leaving the ground bare. The flowers are tubular, and white,
lilac, lavender, or blue, with an orange crest on each fall. They make a very
pretty display. ✿ **PLANTING** The soil for this iris must be rich, moist and
well-drained if they are to grow successfully. Add large quantities of organic
matter in the form of well-rotted manure or compost, and water well until
established. Autumn is the main planting time. ✿ **FLOWERING** Flowers
appear in early spring. ✿ **CULTIVATION** Water well during spring and
summer, and use an general purpose fertilizer after flowering has finished.
Take care to avoid covering the creeping rhizomes with soil or mulch.
✿ **PROPAGATION** Either by division of the rhizomes in late summer or
by seed sown in autumn.

Leucojum aestivum

Summer snowflake ❀ ❖❖❖

❀ **DESCRIPTION** These charming bulbs herald the coming of spring and are very useful for brightening up dark and dreary corners in the garden. The flowers are, as the common name implies, as dainty and intricate as a snowflake with pure-white petals that contrast with the foliage. Each pendent, white bloom is bell shaped, and every petal features a small green spot that is quite distinctive. The strap-shaped leaves reach 20–40 inches (35–50 cm) high, and the bulbs naturalize well under trees, amongst rockeries, or in any shady situation. ❀ PLANTING During autumn, plant the pear-shaped bulbs 2 to 3 inches (5 to 8 cm) deep, into cool, moist, loamy soil, in a position which receives morning sun or soft, dappled light. ❀ **FLOWERING** The white blooms appear in spring. ❀ **CULTIVATION** The summer snowflake is a very easy plant to maintain. Keep the soil moist throughout summer and leave the bulbs undisturbed for several years before lifting and dividing. Protection from frost is not necessary. The spent blooms should be trimmed off during summer and, if necessary, the bulbs divided when all the leaves have completely died back. ❀ **PROPAGATION** By separating bulblets in autumn.

Narcissus sp.
Daffodil ◑ ❖❖❖

❧ **DESCRIPTION** Probably the most popular of all flowering bulbs, the daffodil makes an excellent plant for any semishaded situation, especially in cool climate gardens. The flowers vary considerably according to the variety, from white to deepest yellow. The trumpets also vary in colour and shape, some in beautiful shades of apricot-pink to orange. The stems are erect and hollow, reaching 12–18 inches (30–45 cm) in height, whilst the leaves are dark green and rush-like. There are hundreds of different varieties of daffodil, with flower forms including large cupped, double, miniature and those with reflexed petals. ❧ **PLANTING** Daffodils require a moderately rich, well-drained soil and the bulbs should be planted in autumn for a spring display. For a dramatic effect plant the bulbs in large clumps or drifts, or naturalize them beneath the shade of deciduous trees to create a woodland garden.
❧ **FLOWERING** Blooms anytime from late winter to early spring.
❧ **CULTIVATION** Begin feeding with a balanced fertilizer after the blooms have faded. Allow the bulbs to remain undisturbed for several years until they become congested. When necessary, lift and divide during autumn. Keep the soil moist throughout summer but do not overwater. Daffodils may be attacked by eelworms, the narcissus fly, bulb rot, or rust.
❧ **PROPAGATION** By dividing offsets in autumn.

Ornithogalum umbellatum
Star of Bethlehem ◑ ❖❖❖

❀ **DESCRIPTION** An interesting group of easy-to-grow bulbs, valued for their starry white flowers. They can be used as feature plants in a shaded flowerbed or border garden, or planted in dappled sunlight as a woodland bulb, where they will rapidly multiply and spread. Growing to 1 foot (30 cm), this plant forms an attractive mound of foliage, each leaf being smooth, slender, and mid-green in colour. The flower stalks arise from this mound and are crowned with up to twenty white, star-like flowers, with outer segments striped with green. ❀ **PLANTING** Like many bulbs, star-of-Bethlehem will do well in soil that is well-drained and has been enriched with some well-rotted manure or compost. Choose a sunny or semishaded position, and plant offsets during autumn in well-prepared ground. ❀ **FLOWERING** Flowers appear in mid-spring. ❀ **CULTIVATION** Mulch with leaf litter, and take care not to overwater in summer. Allow the foliage to completely wither and die back after flowering, then sprinkle with an general purpose fertilizer to encourage good flowering the following season. ❀ **PROPAGATION** Easy to propagate from offsets in autumn.

Vallota speciosa (syn. *Cyrtanthus purpureus*)
Scarborough lily ◑ ❖

❀ **DESCRIPTION** This tender bulb, native to South Africa, can be grown successfully in a shaded temperate to warm climate garden, or brought indoors in winter as an attractive houseplant in cooler regions. Growing to 3 feet (1 m) in height, it has handsome, strap-like leaves that are bright green and tall sturdy stems of dramatic funnel-shaped scarlet flowers, which make a wonderful display in autumn. Either indoors or in the garden, it resents direct sunlight on the foliage or flowers. ❀ **PLANTING** To give good results, the soil must be rich and moist yet have prefect drainage. In damp areas create built-up beds or grow in a container that has been lined with stones or broken pieces of terracotta. ❀ **FLOWERING** The flowers appear either in late summer or early autumn. ❀ **CULTIVATION** Water routinely during spring and summer, ensuring that the ground is never waterlogged. Reduce watering after flowering, but don't allow the soil or potting mixture to dry out completely. ❀ **PROPAGATION** From division in early spring.

Aucuba japonica

Japanese aucuba ◑ pH ❖❖

✿ **OTHER NAMES** Japanese laurel, Evergreen spotted laurel

✿ **DESCRIPTION** A hardy, evergreen shrub with a natural, neat habit of compact growth, bearing foliage from the ground up to a height of 9 feet (3 m) with a spread of similar dimensions. The 6 inch (15 cm) shiny green, simple leaves with serrated margins are flecked with yellow, while the cultivars have differing gold-leafed variegations and are generally known as gold dust trees. Grown mainly for its foliage, *Aucuba japonica* is dioecious, so the female plant will only produce bright red berries (sometimes white) if a male plant is growing nearby. It is one of the few variegated plants that will thrive in quite deep shade. ✿ **PLANTING** Once established, these plants will thrive under most conditions, even under trees with established root systems. They can be planted out in spring or autumn, and when planting dig a hole twice the size of the potted plant and fill it with friable, humus-rich loam to help retain moisture. ✿ **FLOWERING** The flowers are rather insignificant, but good forms provide a fine display of berries in winter. ✿ **CULTIVATION** They suit moist, well-drained soils and will benefit from mulching in early stages of growth. ✿ **PROPAGATION** Take half-ripe cuttings in late autumn or early winter, being sure to trim leaves by half to prevent excess transpiration.

Buxus sempervirens

BOX ☉ pH ❖❖❖

❀ **OTHER NAME** Common box ❀ **DESCRIPTION** This popular
plant is commonly used for borders and hedges but also looks good grown
as a specimen pot plant. It is the traditional plant used for topiary work. It
has small, opposing leaves of deep green with brilliant, shiny green new growth
in spring. Eventually growing to 18 feet (6 m), there are many cultivated forms
used for dwarf borders. Worthwhile varieties include 'Suffruticosa', which
will grow to around 3 feet (1 m); var. 'Marginata' is a variegated form with
yellow margin; and var. 'Argentea', with pale yellow variegated leaves, is a
dwarf grower. ❀ **PLANTING** Plant late spring or early summer. Be sure
to dig the soil over well and, if planting a border or hedge, manure evenly to
ensure uniform growth. For a border or hedge, plants should be spaced about
15 inches (35 cm) apart. ❀ **FLOWERING** The small inconspicuous
flowers are held in axillary clusters. ❀ **CULTIVATION** Bushes can be
shaped or trimmed to form a uniform hedge. Clip twice a year, in early to
mid summer and again in autumn, to give a year-round neat appearance.
❀ **PROPAGATION** Hardwood cuttings in late autumn.

Camellia japonica
Common camellia ◑ pH ❖❖

✿ **DESCRIPTION** These delightful shrubs are very easy-to-grow and are ideal for semishaded areas of the garden that have soil that is slightly acidic in its pH level. Plants vary considerably within the *japonica* group, with many growing to an extremely large size, up to 45 feet (15 m) when they reach maturity. In general camellias are large shrubs with a good covering of glossy, deep green foliage and a showy display of waxy flowers that can be single, semi-double, or double and that come in a variety of colours including white, pink, red, or variegated forms. ✿ **PLANTING** Camellias will thrive in moderately rich, moist and slightly acidic soil in a semishaded situation. Afternoon sun is preferable to morning sun, especially for the pale pink or white flowered varieties, which will get scorched petals. Water well until plants are established. ✿ **FLOWERING** Varies according to the variety, generally from late winter to early summer. ✿ **CULTIVATION** Like all shallow-rooted plants, camellias like a good layer of leaf mulch to prevent the soil surface from drying out. Feed annually, when flower buds are forming or immediately after flowering, with a specially formulated camellia fertilizer. Aphids, thrips, and scale insects may cause a problem. ✿ **PROPAGATION** From semiripe cuttings taken in summer or hardwood cuttings taken in winter.

Daphne odora

Winter daphne ⊘ pH ❖❖

✿ **DESCRIPTION** An evergreen shrub to 4 feet (1.25 m), winter daphne is grown for its distinctively fragrant flowers in winter and spring. During the rest of the year its nondescript green foliage tends to blend into the general shrubbery, but it is worth planting in a position where its perfume can be appreciated. The variety 'Alba' has pure-white flowers; var. 'Variegata' has attractive gold-edged leaves. Daphne tends to be short lived, dying off unexpectedly, or it can become leggy; so always have a few cuttings ready to replace the mature plant. ✿ **PLANTING** The main requirement for winter daphne is to be placed in a well-drained position.
✿ **FLOWERING** The clusters of pinkish buds opening to pink and white flowers are prominently displayed at the tips of the branches.
✿ **CULTIVATION** These are surfaced-rooted plants so once established keep mulched to discourage weed growth and keep soil moist. Do not cultivate around the roots as they dislike being disturbed.
✿ **PROPAGATION** Cuttings may be taken from early to mid-summer when the new growth is semi-ripe.

Elaeagnus pungens 'Maculata'

Thorny elaeagnus ◑ pH ❖❖

✿ **DESCRIPTION** This cultivar of *Elaeagnus pungens* is a hardy
evergreen shrub eventually growing to around 10 feet (3 m). The wavy
green, finger-length leaves are normally edged with pale yellow but
sometimes are completely cream; they are dotted brown on the underside
and green above. Requiring little attention, it prefers a sunny position but
will tolerate some shade. Usually grown as part of general shrubbery, it can
be grown as an informal hedge, in which case it will need trimming in late
spring. It is excellent for the shade because its variegated foliage brings
light and brightness to dull areas. ✿ **PLANTING** It is not particular
as to soil type but appreciates well-drained soil and adequate water.
✿ **FLOWERING** Grown more for its foliage, the flowers are insignificant.
✿ **CULTIVATION** Mulch around the plant in autumn and again in
spring, and feed with a general purpose fertilizer in mid growing season.
Occasionally some all-green shoots will appear, and these should be
removed. ✿ **PROPAGATION** Semi-hardwood cuttings, taken towards
the end of summer and layering in spring.

sia hybrids

Fuchsia ◐ ❖

✿ **DESCRIPTION** This large group of plants contains some really delightful flowering varieties, which are easy to cultivate in temperate gardens or under glass, where conditions are cool to cold. They are deciduous or semi-evergreen in habit, losing their foliage only in colder climates when under stress. They can withstand temperatures down to 27°F (–5°C), however they resent very long, hot summers. Fuchsias make excellent plants for containers, which means they are suitable for very cold or very hot climates where they can be moved to shelter when necessary. The flowers and foliage vary considerably according to the variety, however, all the flowers are tubular and pendulous, often with more than one petal shade.

✿ **PLANTING** Plant in a sheltered, semishaded situation in fertile soil that can be kept moist but still has excellent drainage. ✿ **FLOWERING** The flowering period is extensive, from early summer through to late autumn.

✿ **CULTIVATION** Mulch well with organic matter to provide slow-release nutrients and to keep weed growth down. Water well, especially in summer, and stake those varieties where the weight of the flowers drags the stems onto the ground. ✿ **PROPAGATION** Very easily propagated with softwood cuttings taken at any time of the year.

Hydrangea macrophylla

House hydrangea ◑ ❖❖❖

❀ **OTHER NAMES** Hydrangea, Hortensia ❀ **DESCRIPTION** These deciduous, branching shrubs, growing from 18 inches (0.5 m) to 6 feet (2 m), have large heads of flowers offset against attractive deep green leaves with serrated margins, about the size of an open hand. Two forms are generally grown, the common garden or potted form has round heads of sterile flowers, while the 'Lace cap' has flat heads of tiny, fertile flowers in the middle surrounded by a ring of large, sterile ones. ❀ **PLANTING** Hydrangeas are suited to garden or pot culture. Choose a position that receives morning light but is shaded in the afternoon. They need well-drained, sandy loam with ample humus added to provide nutrients to these gross feeders and to hold water, allowing them to cope with the high rate of evaporation through their large leaves. ❀ **FLOWERING** Flowers appear in late spring to early summer. ❀ **CULTIVATION** Hydrangeas range from blue through mauve, to shades of light and dark pink. The shading is governed by the pH of the soil, except for the white flowering types. To alter a blue flowering plant or change a light pink to a deeper pink the soil needs to be made more alkaline. Alternatively, blues are more intense and pinks darker when the soil is acidic. Feed with a general purpose fertilizer in late winter or early spring. Prune after flowering to a pair of plump buds and leave canes that have not flowered. ❀ **PROPAGATION** From hardwood cuttings, about 10 inches (25 cm) long, planted out singly in late autumn.

Kalmia latifolia
Mountain laurel ● ❖❖❖

❀ **OTHER NAMES** American laurel, Calico bush
❀ **DESCRIPTION** Native to the mountainous regions of America, where it can grow up to 25 feet (8 m), it usually reaches 9 feet (3 m) under average garden conditions. An evergreen, it has glossy oval leaves with clusters of dainty, clear pink flowers marked faintly with purple and distinctively crinkled or scalloped at the edges. The cultivar 'Alba' has white flowers. It is a wonderful plant for shady areas so long as proper growing conditions are provided. ❀ **PLANTING** Potted plants from nurseries can be planted out in late autumn or early spring into deep, moist acidic soil. If the soil is depleted, add large quantities of organic matter and water well. ❀ **FLOWERING** Terminal clusters flower in spring.
❀ **CULTIVATION** Mulch in autumn and spring and feed with a general purpose camellia and azalea fertilizer in early spring. No pruning is generally necessary. ❀ **PROPAGATION** Cuttings can be taken in early summer or it can be propagated by layering in spring.

Leucothoe fontanesiana

Drooping leucothoe ◑ pH ❖❖❖

✿ **OTHER NAME** Pearl flower ✿ **DESCRIPTION** An attractive
evergreen pendulous shrub from the southeast of North America. Growing
to around 4 feet (120 cm), it looks good when interplanted with azaleas and
other acid-loving plants of the Erica family. The arching stems have pointed
bronzy green leaves, 4–6 inches (8–15 cm) long. Sprays of lily-of-the-
valley–like flowers hang gracefully towards the end of the shoots, giving rise
to its common name. ✿ **PLANTING** Being fibrous rooted it is best when
planted in late autumn or early spring in a well-drained soil liberally enriched
with humus to ensure moisture retention. ✿ **FLOWERING** Racemes
(sprays) of tightly clustered, tiny white bells are held on the underside of the
branches during spring. ✿ **CULTIVATION** A yearly mulching will ensure
that this surface-rooted plant is kept moist in hot or windy weather and the
need for weeding is reduced. A compact shrub when well attended, it can
tend to become rather open, requiring heavy pruning to ensure new basal
growth. ✿ **PROPAGATION** From semi-hardwood cuttings or seed
taken in late spring. Older plants can provide basal suckers.

Lonicera pileata
Privet honeysuckle ● ❖❖❖

✿ **OTHER NAMES** Honeysuckle ✿ **DESCRIPTION** A low-growing, semi-evergreen shrub that can grow to 3 feet (1 m) with a spread of around 6 feet (2 m), it has small privet-like leaves of glossy green held opposite each other on somewhat stiff, horizontal branches. Ideal for use as a ground cover or for a low hedge, it produces pale yellow flowers followed by masses of small violet berries. A hardy plant that tolerates salt spray, it can be grown in shade where little else will grow. ✿ **PLANTING** Choose a well-drained position and prepare ground by digging over before planting. A liberal dressing of a general purpose fertilizer will ensure good growth in initial stages and the addition of well-rotted manure and compost will help to improve soil texture and retain moisture. ✿ **FLOWERING** Inconspicuous creamy yellow flowers in spring. ✿ **CULTIVATION** Mulch at the beginning of the growing season and again in autumn, and if growing as a hedge, prune lightly each winter to ensure dense, compact growth. ✿ **PROPAGATION** Hardwood cuttings can be taken in winter.

Mahonia japonica

evergrn   ✳

Japanese mahonia   ◑ ● ❖❖

✿ **DESCRIPTION** A useful, upright evergreen shrub for a partially shaded part of the garden, with masses of deep green leaves that consist of many spiny leaflets. The flowers appear in long, spreading sprays and are very fragrant. They are a soft yellow and are followed by attractive purple-blue fruits. Growing to 10 feet (3 m), the shrub has a pleasant rounded shape and makes a good specimen tree because of its attractive foliage, flowers, and fruit. The bark, which is deeply fissured, is also a valued feature of this plant. ✿ **PLANTING** An adaptable plant, the mahonia likes moderately rich and well-drained soils that are not too dry. Add organic matter at planting time, and mulch well to prevent the soil surface from drying out, especially during summer. A semishaded position is preferable. ✿ **FLOWERING** The flowers appear from late autumn to spring, followed by the decorative fruits. ✿ **CULTIVATION** During hot, dry weather deep watering will encourage the downward growth of roots. ✿ **PROPAGATION** From semiripe cuttings taken in summer or from seed collected in autumn.

Mitchella repens

Partridge berry ● ❖❖❖

✿ **OTHER NAME** Two-eyed berry ✿ **DESCRIPTION** A North American woodland native, it has trailing stems that root into the ground. Growing to a height of 15–18 inches (50 cm), the woody branches have almost oval ¾ inch (2 cm) glossy green leaves with whitish veins.

✿ **PLANTING** Like many woodland plants, the partridge berry needs a humus-enriched, moisture retentive soil. Where the soil is dry or depleted, incorporate large quantities of well-rotted compost and manure, and water well until established. ✿ **FLOWERING** Gives tiny funnel-shaped, pinkish white flowers, sometimes tinged with purple in summer, followed by decorative, reddish berries in winter. ✿ **CULTIVATION** A native of sandy, treed areas, the partridge berry appreciates a yearly mulching to provide a cool root run. Water regularly in warm weather.

✿ **PROPAGATION** Rooted branches can be cut from the plant in spring or from ripe berries.

Paeonia suffruticosa
Tree peony ◑ pH ❖❖❖

❀ **OTHER NAME** Mountain peony ❀ **DESCRIPTION** The common
name 'Tree peony' is rather a misnomer as these hardy, deciduous plants
have a shrubby nature. Growing to 6–8 feet (2–2.5 m), they have large,
deeply divided leaves of mid-green arranged alternately along the stems.
They bear white flowers blotched with maroon in spring and cultivars are
available in shades of purple, pink, red, and white, as well as creamy yellow,
in both single and double forms. ❀ **PLANTING** Choose a site that does
not receive morning sun as buds can be damaged by late frost if there is a
quick thaw. Prepare the soil up to 2 feet (60 cm) deep and add a rich humus
mix before placing the plants. ❀ **FLOWERING** Large blooms in spring,
which could benefit from staked supports. ❀ **CULTIVATION** Given a
sheltered position, out the way of winds that could possibly damage new
growth and break the slender stems often holding very large blooms, these
plants benefit from a dressing of bonemeal in late autumn. No pruning is
necessary, however plants benefit from dead-heading and removal of any
damaged wood. ❀ **PROPAGATION** Cultivars are grafted as only the
true species can be reproduced from seed. Layering is possible if access to
well-established plants is available.

Pieris forrestii (syn. *Pieris formosa forrestii*)

Chinese andromeda   ◕ pH ❖❖

✿ **OTHER NAMES** Pearl flower, Andromeda

✿ **DESCRIPTION** A most attractive, dense-foliaged evergreen shrub growing to a height of 6–10 feet (2–3.5 m), with deep green foliage highlighted by rich red, new spring growth. The white lily-of-the-valley–like flowers, held in large panicles, are highlighted against the foliage in tight, light green bud form over winter before opening. ✿ **PLANTING** Having a fibrous root system, these plants do best in a light, humus-enriched soil that is moisture retentive but at the same time well-drained. ✿ **FLOWERING** Flowers in spring. ✿ **CULTIVATION** They prefer a wind-free, sheltered position and benefit from a mulch in autumn and an application of a potash-rich fertilizer in spring. Pruning is not necessary as these plants generally have a naturally compact growth habit. Water routinely, especially in summer if conditions are hot and dry. ✿ **PROPAGATION** Semi-hardwood cuttings taken in late summer when new growth is sufficiently hardened.

Prunus laurocerasus

Cherry laurel ◑ pH ❖❖

✿ **OTHER NAME** English laurel ✿ **DESCRIPTION** One of the few evergreen *Prunus* species, *P. laurocerasus* can grow to 15–20 feet (5–6 m) when planted as a specimen shrub and it is widely used for hedges as it tolerates being clipped. The dark, glossy green leaves are 4 to 6 inches (10–15 cm) long and quite leathery. Fast growing, it has thin panicles of scented white flowers followed by purple-black berries in late summer. There are many varieties freely available including 'Rotundifolia', a rounded form that is useful for hedging; 'Schipkaensis', which is hardier than the others; and 'Zabeliana', which has smaller, neat foliage. ✿ **PLANTING** Prefers deep, moist soil but will perform satisfactorily in ordinary garden loam. If using as a hedge it needs to be planted about 3 feet (1 m) apart. ✿ **FLOWERING** The flowers appear in spring. ✿ **CULTIVATION** Prepare the soil well before planting, adding humus to help with water retention in its early stages. No pruning is necessary if it is growing as a spreading shrub. Used as a hedge or windbreak, it can be trimmed each autumn from 3 to 12 feet (1–4 m). ✿ **PROPAGATION** By seed or semi-hardwood cuttings, which can be taken in summer.

Rhododendron sp.
Azalea ◑ pH ❖❖❖

❖ **DESCRIPTION** The genus *Rhododendron* is divided into over forty individual series, of which azaleas make up a single series. Azaleas are the result of much hybridization between species within this series and can be subdivided into three main groups, namely Indicas, deciduous, and Kurume. The Indicas are evergreen plants ranging in size from 18 inches to 10 feet (50 cm–2.5 m). Cultivars are available in single, semi-double, and double form in white and pink tones. The deciduous types are upright and open in form, ranging in height from 3 to 6 feet (1–2 m), and visually, carry blooms in the yellow, orange, red range. The compact, evergreen Kurume hybrids grow into bushy shrubs 2–3 feet (1 m) high and wide and come in similar tones to the Indicas. ❖ **PLANTING** Indicas thrive in more temperate areas, while the deciduous and Kurume types are better suited to colder areas. All have surface, fibrous roots and benefit from mulching to conserve moisture and keep weeds to a minimum. They are easily transplanted. ❖ **FLOWERING** The spectrum includes all but the blue tones in both single and double, including 'hose-in-hose' forms, and although the main flowering season is spring, cultivars can be obtained to spot bloom almost year round. ❖ **CULTIVATION** Given good drainage and an acidic soil, azaleas are very easy-to-grow in the garden or as potted specimens. For pot culture choose a bowl-shaped container to allow the surface roots as much room as possible and cover the drainage with gravel to permit good drainage. In the garden and especially in tubs do not allow the soil to dry out, particularly in summer. ❖ **PROPAGATION** The evergreen types are easily propagated by semi-hardwood cuttings in early summer or by layering sections of established plants. Deciduous types are propagated from hardwood cuttings.

Rhododendron sp.

Rhododendron ◑ pH ❖❖❖

✿ **DESCRIPTION** A wonderful group of evergreen, cool climate shrubs, which contains many smaller growing varieties that make excellent plants in shady areas of the garden. Although some species grow to 40 feet (14 m), there are many that are 5 feet (1.5 m) or under, and are therefore suitable for gardens of all sizes. Rhododendrons are native to the eastern Himalayas and western China and are valued for their attractive foliage, which is mid-to dark green and sometimes variegated, and the large, showy flowers that are in a wide range of forms and hues. ✿ **PLANTING** Rhododendrons must have soil that is well-drained yet moisture retentive, with an acidic pH level. Incorporate some well-rotted leaf litter and a handful of specially formulated azalea food at the time of planting. Mulch the soil surface with pine bark or a similar organic material. Position in dappled light for the best results.
✿ **FLOWERING** Blooms from late spring onwards, depending on the variety. ✿ **CULTIVATION** Keep the soil lightly damp at all times, especially during hot weather in summer. Dead-head flowers when the blooms have finished. ✿ **PROPAGATION** Either by layering or semi-ripe cuttings taken in late summer.

Ruscus aculeatus

Butcher's broom ◑ ● ❖❖

✿ **DESCRIPTION** This attractive, evergreen plant is particularly valuable
for use in dry, shady areas of the garden where little else will grow. Native to
the southern and western parts of Europe, it grows to 4 feet (1.2 m) in height,
with dense erect stems of glossy dark green leaves and small, star-shaped
greenish flowers that are followed by more showy bright red berries. It is
valued mainly for its handsome foliage, although the berries are also considered
quite appealing. ✿ **PLANTING** This tough and easy-to-grow plant is
suitable for a wide range of soils and climates, and will even survive quite dry
and depleted conditions. However, if care is taken to incorporate additional
well-rotted organic matter at the time of planting, even better results can be
expected. Good drainage is essential, to create built-up beds if the soil is too
heavy or waterlogged. ✿ **FLOWERING** The flowers start appearing in
spring, followed later by the showy fruits. ✿ **CULTIVATION** Once
established little care will be required, apart from thinning out the branches
if they become too dense and crowded, and removal of any dead stems.
This should be done in early spring, before flowering begins.
✿ **PROPAGATION** By division of clumps in early spring.

Sarcococca ruscifolia

Sweet box ◑ ● ❖❖

✿ **OTHER NAME** Fragrant sarcococca ✿ **DESCRIPTION** A small but pretty evergreen shrub that is hardy and easy to cultivate in semi-shaded or shaded parts of the garden. A native of China, it is a member of the Box family and similar in some respects to other species in the group. *Sarcococca ruscifolia* is a compact plant that grows and spreads to 3 feet (1 m). The foliage is dark green and glossy and looks quite attractive even when the plant is not in flower. The flowers are small and creamy white, with a distinctive fragrance. They are followed by scarlet berries that are small but quite showy. The variety 'Chinensis' has slightly more slender leaves. ✿ **PLANTING** Choose a semi-shaded situation and moderately rich, well-drained soil. Incorporate some additional compost and water well, especially when conditions are hot and dry. If drainage is not good, consider growing this plant in a container positioned in the shade. Use a light, well-drained potting mixture. ✿ **FLOWERING** The tiny flowers appear in winter, followed by the berries. ✿ **CULTIVATION** Water in summer, and mulch to prevent the soil drying out too quickly. ✿ **PROPAGATION** From seed sown in autumn, or semi-ripe cuttings taken in summer.

Skimmia japonica
Japanese skimmia ◑ ● ❖❖

❀ **DESCRIPTION** A pleasant evergreen shrub from Japan, which is useful for shady areas of the garden. It grows to 5 feet (1.5 m) in height and spreads about the same with an attractive, dense, rounded outline. The foliage is broadly oval and a rich green, while the flowers are small, white, and starry, borne in dense clusters that make a pretty display. The flowers are followed by large spherical red berries, however, a separate male and female plant will be necessary if these berries are to be obtained.

❀ **PLANTING** Although skimmias grow well in the shade, they resent soil conditions that are dry and depleted, so some preparation will be necessary prior to planting. Ensure that drainage is good, and build up the soil with extra well-rotted compost and manure. Dig quite a large hole, and incorporate the organic matter when the shrub is planted. Water well until established. ❀ **FLOWERING** The flowers appear in late spring, followed by the berries. ❀ **CULTIVATION** Water regularly, especially during hot and dry conditions. Mulch around the base of the plant to keep weed growth down and to help maintain soil moisture. ❀ **PROPAGATION** Either from seed sown in autumn or semi-ripe cuttings taken in late summer.

Viburnum tinus
Laurustinus ○ ◑ ❖❖

✿ **DESCRIPTION** A most attractive evergreen shrub with a dense, bushy habit and a thick covering of oval, deep green foliage. While they can be grown in full sun, they do equally well in semi-shaded situations, especially in areas where the summers are hot and dry. Growing to 10 feet (3.2 m) in height, this species has flat heads of small, white flowers that emerge from pinkish buds covering the entire bush. The variety 'Lucidum' has larger and more showy flowers and a more open growth habit but will not survive harsh growing conditions as easily as the species. Both can be grown in warm and temperate climates but will not survive in areas that experience very cold winters. ✿ **PLANTING** The soil for growing viburnums should be quite rich and well-drained, and capable of holding moisture during hot weather. Add some extra manure or well-rotted compost, and mulch the soil surface to stop the ground from drying out in summer. ✿ **FLOWERING** From late winter through to mid-spring. ✿ **CULTIVATION** Keep well watered in spring and summer, then reduce watering when the cool weather sets in. Prune back in early spring to encourage a more dense shape. ✿ **PROPAGATION** From semi-ripe cuttings taken in autumn.

Vinca major

Greater periwinkle ◑ ● ❖❖❖

✿ **OTHER NAME** Big periwinkle

✿ **DESCRIPTION** A useful and fast-growing evergreen shrub that can be used as a ground cover due to its prostrate habit. It is useful as a spreading plant for shady and partially shady parts of the garden and can be used for both flat areas and steep embankments. The greater periwinkle is a native of Europe and western Asia. Growing to 18 inches (45 cm) in height, it has a good covering of oval, glossy dark green foliage, however the flowers are the most appealing part of the plant, being large, bright blue and very showy. The variety 'Variegata' has bright green leaves with broad creamy white edgings. ✿ **PLANTING** It will grow successfully in any moderately rich and well-drained soil or potting mixture. Add some organic matter to help the soil mix retain moisture during the summer months.

✿ **FLOWERING** Over a long period from late spring until autumn.

✿ **CULTIVATION** Water freely, especially when conditions are hot and dry, and mulch the soil surface to prevent it from drying out.

✿ **PROPAGATION** From semi-ripe cuttings taken in summer or from division of clumps in autumn or early spring.

Vinca minor
Lesser Periwinkle ◑ ● ❖❖❖

✿ **OTHER NAME** Dwarf periwinkle

✿ **DESCRIPTION** A decorative evergreen ground cover for shady parts of the garden, it is ideal for use on steep embankments, beside paths, in rockeries, and under a canopy of trees where few plants will grow. The small, dark green leaves are glossy and mat forming and spread rapidly. During spring or early summer, small trumpet-shaped, lavender-blue flowers appear. Other cultivars have also been developed in shades of white, purple, and navy blue, including a double-flowering variety. This versatile ground cover rarely exceeds 6 inches (15 cm) in height but is capable of spreading up to 10 feet (3 m). ✿ **PLANTING** Choose a shady site with rich, moist soil and ample room to spread. Poorer soils can be improved with the addition of compost and leaf litter to spade depth. Plant during spring or autumn at 2 feet (60 cm) intervals. ✿ **FLOWERING** From mid-spring to early summer. ✿ **CULTIVATION** Very little maintenance is required, except for occasional waterings during the summer months and a dressing of bonemeal or compost each spring. If necessary, the plants may be lightly trimmed after flowering for renewed vigour. If the soil has a tendency to dry out, mulch generously around the plants. ✿ **PROPAGATION** By cuttings or division.

Actinidia chinensis
Chinese gooseberry ◑ pH ❖❖

✿ **OTHER NAMES** Kiwi fruit, Kiwi vine

✿ **DESCRIPTION** A vigorous, woody-stemmed, deciduous twining climber from China that can reach over 30 feet (10 m) in length. Leaves are rough textured and heart shaped. ✿ **PLANTING** Because sexes are carried on different plants it will be necessary to have at least two, and because the male is so much more vigorous than the female, they should be planted at least 15 feet (5 m) apart. One male to eight females is sufficient. Plant where there is shelter from strong winds because young vines are vulnerable to wind damage. ✿ **FLOWERING** Its single nodding white flowers are cup shaped and appear in summer followed by brown, thin-skinned, oval, hairy fruit with edible green flesh that is eaten raw and has a higher vitamin C content than citrus fruit. ✿ **CULTIVATION** Prepare the soil by digging in plenty of bulky organic matter and keep the area weed-free until plants are established. Soil should be well-drained but never allowed to dry out. Prune in winter if necessary. ✿ **PROPAGATION** Propagate from seed sown in spring or autumn, or by semi-ripe cuttings in midsummer, or by layering in winter. It is best to buy grafted male and female plants because it may be many years before the sex of seedlings is known.

evergrn

Allamanda cathartica
Golden trumpet ◑ pH ❖

❀ **DESCRIPTION** This fast-growing woody-stemmed, evergreen scrambling climber has a milky sap and carries whorls of glossy, lance-shaped leaves. It is best known, however, for its trumpet-shaped, bright yellow flowers which grow 3-4 inches (7-10cm) across.

❀ **PLANTING** Choose a warm, sheltered spot, preferably beside a wall and supply supports so that the stems can be tied to them as they grow. The soil should be moderately fertile with good drainage, yet capable of holding moisture, especially during summer. If the area is dry or depleted, incorporate plenty of organic matter in the form of well-rotted compost or manure. ❀ **FLOWERING** Flowers appear from summer to autum. ❀ **CULTIVATION** Feed and water regularly, particularly when in full growth, but allow the soil to be on the dry side in late autumn when the growth ceases. Mulch with leaf litter, which will also improve pH levels. ❀ **PROPAGATION** Propagate by softwood cuttings in spring or summer.

Hedera canariensis

Algerian ivy ● ṗH ❖❖

✿ **OTHER NAME** Canary Island ivy ✿ **DESCRIPTION** A vigorous evergreen climber, clinging with aerial roots. Heart-shaped or three-lobed leaves are dark glossy green with pale green veins and can be up to 6 inches (15 cm) across. Stems and leaf stalks are deep red. From the Canary Islands, Madeira, and North Africa. Can reach 18 feet (6 m) when grown in the right conditions. ✿ **PLANTING** Often used as a ground cover and to hold embankments but can be used to cover walls and trellises and will establish more quickly than some other ivies. Bright light but not direct sunlight is best, except for variegated forms, which need some sunlight daily to retain their variegation. The soil should be moderately rich, moist, and well-drained. ✿ **FLOWERING** Clusters of small, pale green insignificant flowers are followed by fleshy berries in summer and autumn. ✿ **CULTIVATION** Best in temperate and subtropical areas and prefers a damp site. Prune in spring. Keep well watered during the growing season, particularly if temperatures are high and the air is dry. Apply liquid feed every two weeks during the growing season. The red spider mite could be a problem when grown indoors in hot, dry rooms. Prune away weak growth to encourage branching. ✿ **PROPAGATION** By cuttings of firm young shoots or rooted layers.

Hedera helix

Ivy   ● p̂H ❖❖❖

✿ **OTHER NAMES** Common ivy, English ivy

✿ **DESCRIPTION** A vigorous evergreen root clinger with five-lobed dark green leaves up to 3 inches (7 cm) long. There are distinct juvenile and adult growth phases. In the juvenile phase the stems form clinging roots freely and the leaves are deeply lobed. In the adult phase, which usually develops when the plant reaches the top of its support, stem roots are rarely produced and the leaves become rounded and less noticeably lobed. Can reach 30 feet (10 m). The ornamental cultivars are very popular. ✿ **PLANTING** Best used as a trailing plant in hanging baskets because it can become invasive when used as a ground cover. Can be grown in quite poor, dry soil; however, better results are achieved if the area is first prepared with some organic matter. ✿ **FLOWERING** Clusters of greenish, insignificant flowers are followed by fleshy black berries. ✿ **CULTIVATION** Widely grown as a ground cover or as a self-clinging climber on brickwork. Also useful as a decorative plant in pots indoors in well-lit areas. It is easily grown in a variety of positions but likes plenty of moisture. ✿ **PROPAGATION** By cuttings of firm young wood.

Hydrangea anomala ssp. *petiolaris*

Climbing hydrangea ◐ pH ❖❖❖

✿ **DESCRIPTION** A deciduous, woody-stemmed aerial root climber with toothed, glossy green leaves up to 5 inches (12 cm) long. Lacy-headed small white flowers are produced in domed, terminal bunches which can reach up to 8 inches (20 cm) across. From Asia, the climbing hydrangea can grow up to 45 feet (15 m). ✿ **PLANTING** This climber can be trained over a wall or a tree stump and grows best in temperate regions. The soil should be moderately rich, moist, and well-drained, with plenty of organic matter added prior to planting. ✿ **FLOWERING** The flowers appear during summer only. ✿ **CULTIVATION** The climbing hydrangea prefers fertile, moist soil. Prepare the ground prior to planting, and water well, especially during the main growing season if conditions are hot and dry. ✿ **PROPAGATION** Hardwood cuttings are best taken during winter.

evergreen

Lapageria rosea
Chilean bellflower ◑ pH ❖

❁ **OTHER NAME** Copihue ❁ **DESCRIPTION** An evergreen woody-stemmed, twining climber reaching 15 feet (5 m), with 2–3 inch (5 cm) leathery leaves. It is the national flower of Chile. Pruned to shape, it can be grown in a glasshouse in cold climates and moved outdoors for summer display. ❁ **PLANTING** Plant in humus-rich, well-drained soil and supply a fine support for it to climb on. If the soil is depleted add plenty of organic matter in the form of well-rotted compost or manure. ❁ **FLOWERING** *Lapageria rosea's* pendent pink to red trumpet flowers have a fleshy texture, are 3 inches (8 cm) long with pale flecks, appear from summer to late autumn, and are followed by a many-seeded berry. The three outer petals are longer than the three inner petals. ❁ **CULTIVATION** Water moderately and even less when not in full growth. Thin out congested growth in spring. ❁ **PROPAGATION** From seed sown in spring after soaking for two days, also by layering and cuttings.

Lonicera caprifolium
Italian honeysuckle ◐ pH ❖❖❖

✿ **OTHER NAME** Italian woodbine ✿ **DESCRIPTION** A vigorous, deciduous woody-stemmed climber growing to 15 feet (5 m) with dull green, 4 inch (10 cm) leaves in pairs. The bases of the upper leaves unite to form a little cup. ✿ **PLANTING** Plant where the soil will be well watered and supply a support or clip the plant into a shrub. Prepare the ground well before planting by adding plenty of well-rotted compost or manure. ✿ **FLOWERING** Richly fragrant, tubular, creamy yellow flowers are tinged with pink on the outside of the petals and borne in spring at the ends of branches. ✿ **CULTIVATION** Prune after flowering to remove the dead stems and old flowering wood and keep watch for aphids in spring. ✿ **PROPAGATION** By seed in autumn or spring or by cuttings in summer or late autumn.

Quisqualis indica

Rangoon creeper ◑ pH ❖

❀ **DESCRIPTION** An evergreen twining and scrambling climber, with thin-textured, light green 4 inch (10 cm) leaves, reaching 30 feet (10 m) or more. Originally from tropical South-East Asia, it can be grown under glass in cool climates if pruned to control height and spread. The plants can be moved outdoors for summer interest in the garden, or can be grown in the garden as annuals. The starry, five-petalled flowers are about an inch (3 cm) across, held in clusters on long, thin tubes and are fragrant at night. White at first, they age to salmon-pink and brick-red and are followed by decorative black fruit. ❀ **PLANTING** Needs fertile, moist but well-drained soil and copious amounts of water during the warm growing season. Prior to planting, incorporate some additional organic matter to the soil, either well-rotted compost or manure. ❀ **FLOWERING** The showy flowers appear from late spring to autumn. ❀ **CULTIVATION** It may grow prolifically in tropical and subtropical areas, so thin out the crowded growth in spring as needed. ❀ **PROPAGATION** By seed in spring or semi-ripe cuttings in summer.

Ageratum houstonianum

Ageratum ◑ p̂H

✿ **OTHER NAME** Floss flower ✿ **DESCRIPTION** This is a mounding, fast-growing annual from Central America. *Ageratum houstonianum's* delightful clusters of feathery, powder-puff–like flowers are mostly blue or mauve but are occasionally found in pink or white. The leaves are oval, pale green, and somewhat hairy. Tall cultivars can reach up to 2 feet (60 cm), while dwarf cultivars grow to only 6 inches (15 cm). ✿ **PLANTING** *Ageratum houstonianum* grows best in quite fertile, well-drained soil. It looks wonderful planted as an edging plant or at the front of a mixed flowerbed or border. For best results, incorporate some extra organic matter prior to planting. ✿ **FLOWERING** Flowers appear in summer and autumn. ✿ **CULTIVATION** Regular watering and fertilizing will increase the flowering season and continuous flowering is possible during the season if the plants are dead-headed regularly. ✿ **PROPAGATION** By seed in spring.

perer.

Bellis perennis

Daisy ◐ pH

✿ **OTHER NAME** English daisy ✿ **DESCRIPTION** A popular and easy-to-grow carpeting plant that will adapt to a wide range of soils and conditions. Although a perennial plant in temperate regions, it is most commonly grown as an annual in cooler areas. It reaches a height of 4–6 inches (12–15 cm) and can withstand light frost and drought. There are single, semi-double, and double forms in shades of white, pink, and dark red, with yellow centres. Leaves are mid-green, oval in shape, and slightly hairy. Best effects are achieved by mass-planting in borders or rockeries. The original *Bellis perennis* species is a troublesome lawn daisy and is not sold in nurseries. It has been surpassed by less-invasive cultivars, which are superior as garden plants.✿ **PLANTING** Grow in full sun to semi-shade in fertile, moist, and well-drained soil. Poor soil will be tolerated, so long as it is well drained. Plant during spring into soil that has been supplemented with organic matter. Keep snails and weeds at bay while the plant is established. ✿ **FLOWERING** Flowers abundantly through late spring and summer. ✿ **CULTIVATION** Water well in dry spells, and mulch around plants to prevent the soil surface from drying out. ✿ **PROPAGATION** Sow seed outdoors in mild areas during late spring or summer, or sow in punnets under glass from early spring. Plants can also be divided in autumn, after flowering.

Coleus x *hybridus*

Flame nettle ◗ pH

✿ **DESCRIPTION** The flame nettle is a fast-growing perennial that is grown as an annual in cooler regions. It reaches 20 inches (50 cm) in height with serrated leaves of various shapes, from oval and unlobed to long and deeply lobed. The leaves are found in pink, apricot, raspberry, yellow, green, and a variety of mixtures of these. Originally from the tropics of Asia, there are now many hybrids of *Coleus*. ✿ **PLANTING** The flame nettle makes a useful pot plant for partial shade in the garden and is also often used as an indoor plant. It will grow best in fertile, well-drained soil. ✿ **FLOWERING** Spikes of tiny mauve flowers appear in summer and should be removed to encourage the plant to thicken.
✿ **CULTIVATION** Keep this plant well watered and pinch out growing shoots of young plants to encourage branching. ✿ **PROPAGATION** By seed in late winter or by softwood cuttings in spring or summer.

Impatiens 'New Guinea hybrids'

Balsam ◑ pH

✿ **OTHER NAMES** Busy Lizzy, Impatiens ✿ **DESCRIPTION** This group includes annuals, perennials, and subshrubs that can reach 20 inches (50 cm), often with succulent but brittle stems. Pointed, oval-shaped burgundy to bronze-green leaves are sometimes variegated in yellow or white. In colder regions, they can be grown as potted plants in the glasshouse or on a sheltered balcony, planted after all danger of frost has passed, and moved outdoors for a colourful display in the garden during the warmer months. ✿ **PLANTING** Plant in moist but well-drained soil in the garden. The compact growth habit of the smaller hybrids means that they can be successfully used as border plants. This group is also suited to large containers or hanging baskets. ✿ **FLOWERING** The flat, five-petalled flowers are spurred and can be pink, orange, flame red, cerise, coral, or salmon. They sometimes appear with white blotches and are held close above the foliage. In warm climates they appear year round, but in temperate areas from spring to autumn only. ✿ **CULTIVATION** In mild climates they are perennial but in cold climates they are herbaceous. Feed every two weeks during the long flowering period and never allow them to dry out. Beware of red spider mites and aphids when cultivating indoors. ✿ **PROPAGATION** By seed or stem cuttings during warm weather.

Lunaria annua

Honesty ● pH˯

✿ **OTHER NAME** Money plant ✿ **DESCRIPTION** The perfumed,
four-petalled white to deep purple flowers of *Lunaria annua* are followed
by flat, round satiny seed cases that give this plant much of its charm.
Although it can be grown as a biennial and even as a perennial in some
regions, it is generally grown as an annual in cool to cold climates. *Lunaria
annua* is fast-growing, erect, and has pointed, somewhat oval, serrated
leaves. Some can reach 3 feet (1 m) in height. ✿ **PLANTING** This
charming plant needs well-drained soil and is suitable for planting in full to
partial shade. ✿ **FLOWERING** Flowers appear in spring and early
summer. *Lunaria annua* will sometimes flower in the first year.
✿ **CULTIVATION** Keep well fed and watered especially during the main
growing period of spring and summer, or if conditions are hot and dry.
✿ **PROPAGATION** By seed in autumn or spring.

Myosotis sylvatica

Forget-me-not ◑ pH

❧ **DESCRIPTION** Forget-me-nots are delightful, hardy plants, suitable for planting in most parts of the garden and are especially effective in a rockery. This plant is mostly grown for the attractive flowers which are small, flat, and five-petalled, and are held above the leaves on fine branchlets. The flowers are mostly sky-blue but sometimes come in pink or white, and have a yellow eye. The leaves are narrow and hairy. An erect annual or biennial, *Myosotis* grows to 2 feet (60 cm). These charming plants are very easy to grow and will self-seed freely all over the garden, including those shady places where little else will grow. They are great space fillers between other annuals, perennials, and shrubs. ❧ **PLANTING** Forget-me-nots will grow best in moist, fertile, well-drained soil; however, they will survive in quite poor soils, and even dry situations. ❧ **FLOWERING** Flowers appear from spring to autumn. ❧ **CULTIVATION** After flowering, plants often get powdery mildew so are best removed. ❧ **PROPAGATION** By seed, which is produced in great abundance, sown in autumn.

iana alata (syn. *Nicotiana affinis*)

owering tobacco ◑

❀ **DESCRIPTION** This attractive rosette-forming perennial is generally
grown as an annual in temperate to cold climates, making a pleasant display
at the back of a mixed flower bed or border. Growing to 3 feet (1 m) or
more in height, it has mid-green oval leaves and clusters of tubular creamy
white flowers which exude a pleasant fragrance in the evening. There is also
a green form, 'Lime Green', which has a similar growth habit although it is
slightly more compact. The 'Sensation series' has pointed leaves and rose or
crimson flowers. ❀ **PLANTING** Position in a container or directly in the
ground in a semi-shady part of the garden, and ensure that the soil or potting
mixture is moderately rich, moist, and well drained. If growing from seed,
plants can be raised to the seedlings stage in punnets, then transplanted into
larger pots when 6 inches (15 cm) in height. Sow seeds in spring in cool to
cold climates, or in autumn in warmer regions. ❀ **FLOWERING** Flowers
from summer to early autumn, depending on when the seeds were sown.
❀ **CULTIVATION** Keep water to these plants, especially during spring
and summer if conditions are hot and dry. A feed of liquid organic
fertilizer after six weeks' growth will help to boost flower production.
❀ **PROPAGATION** From seed sown in autumn or spring, depending
on the climate.

Nigella damascena
Love-in-a-mist ❧

❀ **DESCRIPTION** An easy-to-grow, pretty annual that is a member of
the Buttercup family and native to southern Europe. It grows well in full
sun but can also create a pretty display in dappled shade. It is a popular and
fast-growing species, reaching 18 inches (50 cm) in height, with slender
upright stems clothed in fine, feathery bright green foliage. The spurred
flowers are small semi-doubles in shades of blue, pink, and white.
Worthwhile varieties include 'Miss Jekyll', which has semi-double blue
flowers; and 'Persian jewels', which has white, pink, or purple-blue flowers.
The flowers are followed by decorative seed pods, which can be allowed to
dry to provide seed for the following season. ❀ **PLANTING** This annual
grows well in most soils and climates, providing drainage is adequate. Add
some organic matter to the ground prior to sowing the seeds, and keep the
area lightly moist until germination. ❀ **FLOWERING** Love-in-a-mist
blooms during late spring and early summer. ❀ **CULTIVATION** Weed
around the young seedlings as they grow, and mulch to help keep the soil
moist. Dead-heading will encourage more flowers to be produced.
❀ **PROPAGATION** In cool climates seed is sown in spring when the
danger of frost has passed; in other regions seed is sown in autumn.

Reseda odorata

Mignonette

✿ **DESCRIPTION** A most attractive old-fashioned annual that can be grown to great effect in semishaded situations. A native of Africa, this plant is fast growing with a pleasant, branching shape and masses of mid-green foliage topped by conical heads of starry white flowers with a delightful fragrance. The flowers have orange stamens, which are quite prominent. There are dwarf varieties available. ✿ **PLANTING** This annual is best grown directly from seed, as it resents being transplanted at seedling stage. Choose a shaded situation and prepare the ground with some additional organic matter before scattering the seeds on the surface, then covering with a layer of fine soil or seed-raising mixture. Keep lightly moist until the seeds have germinated. Spring is the best time to sow.

✿ **FLOWERING** Mignonette flowers in summer or autumn, depending on when the seed was sown. The flowers are good for cutting for indoor floral arrangements. ✿ **CULTIVATION** Maintain watering, especially during spring and summer if conditions are dry. Remove spent flowers to extend the flowering period. ✿ **PROPAGATION** From seed sown in spring, when the danger of frost has passed.

Torenia fournieri

Wishbone flower

✿ **OTHER NAME** Blue torenia ✿ **DESCRIPTION** A pretty annual
that can be grown in a semi-shaded situation, bringing colour to areas of
the garden that may otherwise be drab and dreary. In cooler climates it
can be potted and brought indoors to make a lovely display in autumn. A
native of China, it grows to 1 foot (30 cm) in height, and has a branching
habit and pale green leaves with serrated edges. Quite a fast grower, it
produces very attractive deep purple-blue flowers with pale yellow and
white centres. ✿ **PLANTING** An easy-to-grow plant that will tolerate a
wide range of soils and conditions but prefers moderately rich, moist, and
well-drained ground. It can be cultivated from seed sown in spring,
directly where the plants are to grow, or from seedlings that have been
raised under glass and transplanted into the garden when the danger of
frost has passed. ✿ **FLOWERING** Flowers from summer to early autumn.
✿ **CULTIVATION** Water regularly, especially in spring and summer if
the weather becomes hot and dry. Pinch out the shoots of plants when
young, as this will encourage a more compact, bushy growth habit.
✿ **PROPAGATION** From seed sown in spring.

INDEX OF BOTANICAL NAMES

INDEX OF COMMON NAMES

PHOTOGRAPHY CREDITS

INDEX OF COMMON NAMES